BRITISH TRAMCAR MANUFACTURERS

BRITISH WESTINGHOUSE AND METROPOLITAN-VICKERS

BY DAVID VOICE

PUBLISHED BY ADAM GORDON

ALSO BY DAVID VOICE

How to Go Tram and Tramway Modelling
London's Tramways and How to Model Them
What Colour was that Tram?
Tramway Modelling in 'OO' Gauge
More Tramway Modelling in 'OO' Gauge
The Illustrated History of Kidderminster and Stourport Electric Tramway Company (with Melvyn Thompson)
How to Go Tram and Tramway Modelling, 2nd edition
The Millennium Guide to Trams in the British Isles
The Definitive Guide to Trams in the British Isles, 2nd edition
The Definitive Guide to Trams in the British Isles, 3rd edition
Toy and Model Trams of the World, Volume 1: Toys, Die-casts and Souvenirs (with Gottfried Kuře)
Toy and Model Trams of the World, Volume 2: Plastic, White Metal and Brass (with Gottfried Kuře)
Next Stop Seaton! (with David Jay)
How to Go Tram and Tramway Modelling, 3rd edition
Hospital Tramways and Railways, 1st, 2nd and 3rd editions
Freight on Street Tramways in the British Isles

FRONT COVER PHOTOS
In 1904 British Westinghouse succeeded in winning the substantial contract for 200 tramcars ordered by London County Council. Number 208, a Class C tramcar, was part of the order. Originally open top, the balcony cover was added later by LCC.

BACK COVER PHOTOS
Left:
The British Westinghouse water tower was the best known feature of the Trafford Park factory. It was demolished in the Second World War to prevent it being used as a navigation marker by enemy aircraft.
Top right:
The factory, when owned by Metropolitan Vickers, with workers streaming out at the end of the day, over Taylor's Bridge on the Bridgewater Canal.
Middle upper right:
In the First World War the War department ordered 100 of these petrol electric locomotives from British Westinghouse. They were originally ordered as trolley pole operated electric tram locomotives.
Middle lower right:
Tramcar controllers manufactured at the Trafford Park factory – on the left by British Westinghouse and on the right by Metropolitan Vickers.
Bottom right:
To open their tramway in 1905, Walthamstow Corporation purchased 32 open-top tramcars all fitted with Westinghouse electrical equipment. This is number 20 at the Napier Arms terminus.

© David Voice 2008

All rights reserved. No part of this publication may be reproduced, stored in a retrieval system or transmitted in any form or by any means electronic, mechanical, photocopying, recording or otherwise, without prior permission in writing from the author David Voice.

British Library Cataloguing in Publication Data
Voice, David

ISBN
978 1 874422 68 6

Publication no.72

Published in 2008 by Adam Gordon, Kintradwell Farmhouse, Brora, Sutherland KW9 6LU
Tel 01408 622660
E-mail: adam@ahg-books.com

Printed by 4Edge Ltd, Hockley, Essex SS5 4AD
First printing limited to 400 copies
Production by Trevor Preece (epic_trev@epic-gb.com)

Contents

BRITISH TRAMCAR MANUFACTURERS
BRITISH WESTINGHOUSE AND METROPOLITAN-VICKERS

Introduction		4
Chapter 1	George Westinghouse	7
Chapter 2	British Westinghouse	17
Chapter 3	The Tramway Products of British Westinghouse and Metrovick	31
Chapter 4	Controllers and Motors	37
Chapter 5	Brakes	49
Chapter 6	First World War Tramcars	61
Chapter 7	Trafford Park Tramways	63
Chapter 8	Metropolitan Vickers Electrical Company Limited	69
Chapter 9	The Decline and Fall of George Westinghouse	79
Appendix 1	Companies Established by George Westinghouse	84
Appendix 2	Surviving Westinghouse and Metrovick controllers	85
Appendix 3	Motors of Westinghouse and Metrovick	88
Appendix 4	British Tramway Systems using Westinghouse/Metrovick equipment	89
Appendix 5	Westinghouse in France	104
Acknowledgements		104
Key to abbreviations		105
Bibliography		106

Introduction

This all started when I read John Price's book "The Dick, Kerr Story". I had for some time admired the series of books on the British tramcar manufacturers researched and written by John. So it was with a tinge of sadness that I read at the end of the Dick, Kerr book that future books would have to be left to others. I contacted John some time later (rather hoping that others would have taken up the challenge). However, I was told that no-one else had come forward. So I volunteered, expecting to take on the English Electric story identified in the book. John had other ideas and suggested that I focused on British Westinghouse and Metrovick. Since I knew as little about this as about English Electric I was happy to take it on.

John gave me invaluable pointers and information and I set about looking for more. The first task was to reconstruct the order book for tramcar orders. Alas no records are known of the order books. So I reconstructed it using information on all the tramway systems in the country and some from abroad. At the same time I started to read all I could about British Westinghouse and Metrovick. I found a fascinating story. I hope that I have been able to convey some of the complex and involved story behind the man, his organisation, as well as of the products. As my interest is solely to do with tramways I have ignored the other products, many connected to electrical generation or operating equipment. In reality the tramway component of the business was a very minor aspect of a massive organisation, but it did bring in much needed revenue.

This book records the tramway business of the British Westinghouse Company and its successor Metropolitan Vickers. In view of the major contribution the company made to tramway braking, I have also explored in more detail this aspect of tramway safety. Indeed tramway travel was and still is a very safe method of transport. With the tramcar travelling on rails, the pedestrians are aware of where the tram will go and can be confident of when they are safe. Indeed this is well demonstrated in many continental towns where trams are allowed in pedestrianised areas. I well remember being in Dusseldorf and amazed to see a long articulated tram driving at 10-15 mph through a packed pedestrian area. The crowds just parted to allow the tram through as normally as passing another pedestrian.

Tramcars fitted with British Westinghouse electrical equipment: Douglas Southern, London County Council, Coventry Corporation and Bath Tramways.

Today there is little that remains of British Westinghouse. The Trafford Park Industrial Estate has long gone, there is virtually no British tramcar indus-

Tramcars fitted with Metropolitan Vickers electrical equipment: Edinburgh Corporation, Glasgow Corporation, Leeds Corporation, London County Council no. 1, London County Council, Sheffield Corporation. (British Westinghouse, Tramway and Light Railway Society Archive)

try and the new generation of tramways in Birmingham, Croydon, Manchester and Sheffield all use tramcars built abroad. Today the only British-built trams in public service are at Blackpool, the Isle of Man, Seaton and Southport Pier.

David Voice, January 2008

This book is dedicated to the late John Price, tramway historian, founder member of the National Tramway Museum and author of many tramway books and articles, including the first six volumes of the history of British tramcar manufacturers. John was a fount of tramway information and he was always willing to share his knowledge with others. It was his enthusiasm and generosity with his own researches that led to this book being written.

"Knowledge is of no value unless it is shared with others."
Vane A. Jones; Editor of *Traction and Models* magazine

Chapter 1

GEORGE WESTINGHOUSE
6 OCTOBER 1846 – 12 MARCH 1914

The beginnings of British Westinghouse are part of the story of the rise of George Westinghouse. A larger than life character, George Westinghouse had ambitions to develop the use of electrical power further than any other person in the world. His life demonstrates the enormous personal energy he had. He single-handedly created a vast international empire of companies. However, not all his visions were correct and his ambitions outstripped reality. The outcome, as far as British Westinghouse was concerned, was rejection and a lack of any formal recognition for his achievements.

George Westinghouse was born in a small village called Central Bridge, New York, USA. His great-great-grandmother had emigrated to America in 1755 from the Westphalian area of Germany. She was a widow and was accompanied by her son John Hendrik, then aged 15. Their name at that time was probably Wistinghausen, which became changed to the more American Westinghouse. They settled in Pownal, Bennington County in the Vermont mountains, acquiring land and building a log cabin. John married and raised a large family, including John Ferdinand, George's grandfather. John stayed in Pownal raising his own family, the fifth child being named George, George's father. This George married Emaline Vedder and had ten children, of whom George Westinghouse was the eighth.

In 1860, at the age of thirteen and a half George started work in his father's engineering shop in Schenectady, which had been set up in 1856. The shop manufactured agricultural machinery including grain threshing machines, steam engines and steam traction engines. By a quirk of fate George Westinghouse's fiercest competitor, General Electric (GE), was later to set up its factory in Schenectady, next door to his father's shop. In 1860 his pay was 50 cents a day. When the Civil War broke out George was 15 and he ran away to enlist. His father acted promptly to halt his military career and he returned home to carry on working in the engineering shop. However, two years later he was allowed to go to war as an enlisted man.

An advertisement from the agricultural engineering company owned by George Westinghouse senior (George's father). (Author's collection)

George Westinghouse in 1884 at the age of 38. (Tramway and Light Railway Society Archive)

George Westinghouse in the latter years, with his signature. (Tramway and Light Railway Society Archive)

He served in the infantry and cavalry for a short time before becoming an engineer officer in the navy. He returned from service in the navy in 1865 and rejoined his father's engineering shop. His father had patented seven inventions, so it is not surprising that son George should have inherited an aptitude for inventing.

George took out his first patent for a rotary steam engine in 1865 at the age of 19. This proved impractical, but it did not stop him from continuing to apply his active mind. In the same year he obtained a patent for re-railing railway freight cars. This led to the setting up of a small engineering shop in Schenectady. Then he was offered the job of travelling salesman for Anderson and Cook, a steel manufacturer in Pittsburgh. They had agreed to manufacture his re-railer and his task was to sell it. At the age of twenty he married Marguerite Erskine Walker after a whirlwind romance. They were engaged three days after first meeting on a train and the wedding soon followed on 8th August 1867. The marriage lasted until his death in 1914 and he always said that all his successes were due to his wife.

A few years after his marriage he made his first major invention. This was the railway air brake. At this time the main effort of railway companies had been in making their trains go faster, with little regard as to how to stop them. In England many express passenger trains only had braking on the engine. A series of bad

George Westinghouse with the Directors of one of the French companies set up by him. (Tramway and Light Railway Society Archive)

accidents, made all the more serious by the unchecked momentum of following carriages ploughing into the wreckage, made the railway companies pay more attention to safety. At that time the instructions to engine drivers was that in emergency they should put the engine into reverse and spin the wheels backwards as fast as possible. In America goods covered vans had the brake wheel fitted at roof level, requiring a brakeman to ride on top of the vans. On passenger trains there would be several guards' vans among the carriages and the guards would apply the brakes in response to whistles from the engine driver. It is said that a head-on collision between two trains on the railway between Schenectady and Troy in 1866 prompted George to put his mind to the problem of railway braking. Apparently a human error had put the two trains approaching each other on the same line. The speeds were not high and there was ample warning, but the braking systems were so poor that the trains collided causing enormous damage. After some false starts with chain brakes, leading to thoughts on steam braking, he happened on an article which described compressed air drills operated by compressors some 3000 feet away. He realised that the power of the compressed air could be used to activate the brakes along the whole of the train. Thus he invented the air brake which worked on all carriages and wagons in the train at the same time. The train driver activated a lever that allowed compressed air into the braking system and the pres-

Part of the Westinghouse American Empire. (Author's collection)

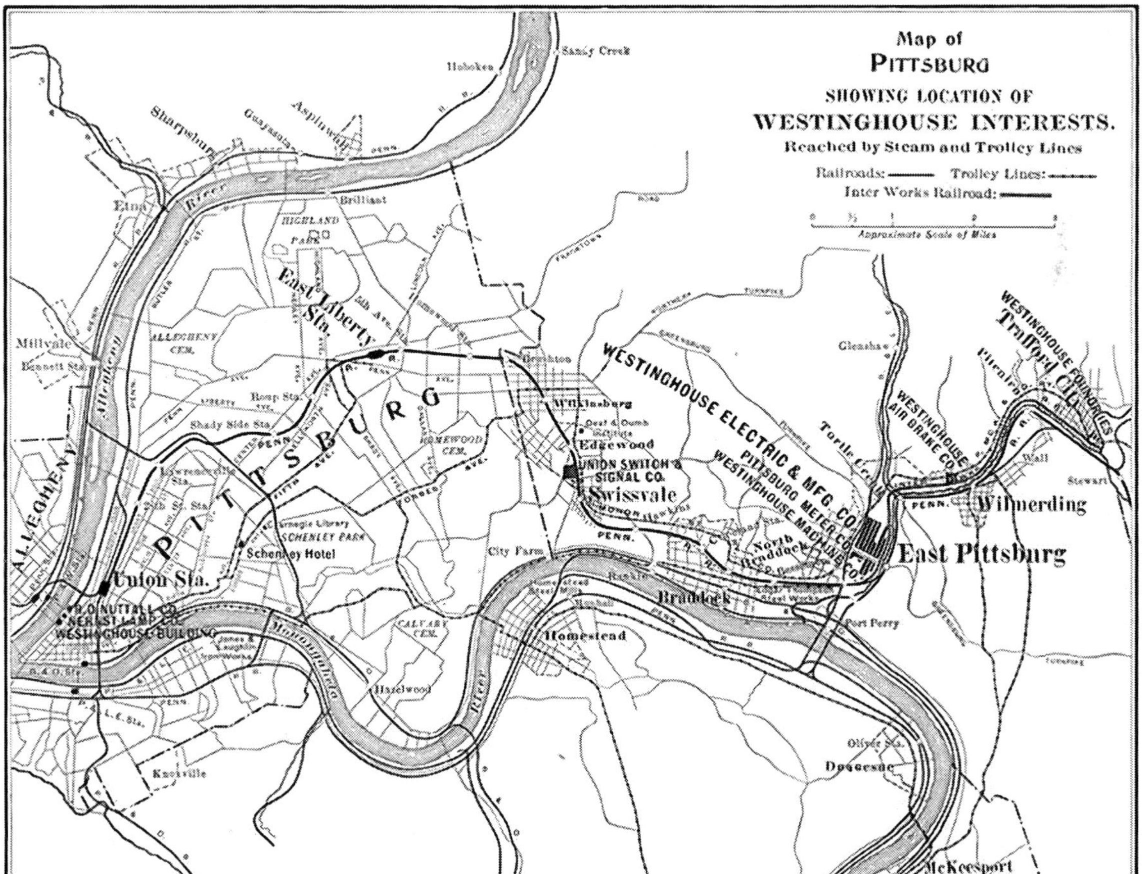

Pittsburgh showing the many Westinghouse factories located in the city. (Author's collection)

sure operated the brakes. Initially it was rejected by the railroad industry as impractical. George had funding difficulties – even his own father refused to give him funds and told him to get more practical employment. George had plenty of contacts in the railroad industry with his sales of his re-railer. So he would promote his air brake ideas at the same time. But it was not until a Mr W.W. Card, superintendent in the Panhandle Railroad, was told of the idea that progress was made. Mr Card arranged for the railroad to test the system, but George had to pay for the test and bear all the risks. He persuaded a friend, Ralph Baggaley, to back the project financially. During the run of the test train, as it emerged from a tunnel, a horse and cart was crossing the track. The cart driver spurred his horse on, but it shied and threw him on to the track. The brakes were applied in emergency and the train halted before reaching the cart driver – an unexpected test of the brakes that proved their effectiveness. The railroad agreed to purchase the braking system. So the Westinghouse Air Brake Company was established with George Westinghouse as President and Ralph Baggaley as Vice President and W.W. Card as General Agent. The year was 1869 and George was just 23 and embarking on his engineering empire. Soon air brakes were being installed on many of the railways of the USA. The major fault of this 'straight' air brake was that if the train split, the pipe connecting the rolling stock would snap and all braking would be lost. This was later remedied by applying the brakes using strong springs, or later air pressure from pressurised reservoirs on each vehicle, and the train air pressure kept the brakes off the wheels. So a reduction in that air pressure applied the braking.

Ever one to seize the opportunity George Westinghouse paid his first visit to England in 1871. He spent his time advertising his air brake system and trying to sell it to the British railway companies. His reception is summed up in the words of a railway manager of the time, who when asked why he had not adopted the Westinghouse brake replied "Sir, I am an Englishman". This was an attitude that led to further fatalities on British railways and that dogged his dealings in Britain. These prejudices still had an influence on British Westinghouse even as late as 1916.

During his stay in England he wrote to the *"Engineer"* about his air brake. One of the editors, John Dredge, printed what he believed to be the fundamental elements of a safe braking system for railways. This included all carriages being automatically braked should a train split. At this time the Westinghouse system did not do this. George Westinghouse took back these ideas and by 1872 he had perfected the Westinghouse Automatic Air Brake, which met all the requirements. This was a great success and in 1893 an Act made such air brakes compulsory on all USA trains. A major innovation at the time was the decision to standardise all his air brake equipment to enable apparatus on wagons of different lines to work together and that improved designs would work with earlier models. This pioneering work in standardisation has received little recognition.

His second visit to England came in 1874. By then the straight air braking system had been used on several railways. The purpose of the second visit was to promote the automatic air brake. Here he found that Hodge's vacuum brake was a serious competitor, so when he returned to the States he bought out the Hodge patent and then promptly offered railways either vacuum or air braking systems.

In Britain there was concern over the number of deaths caused by railway accidents. In 1875 a Royal Commission arranged with railway companies to undertake experiments lasting a week with continuous braking systems at Newark. The result showed that continuous braking was very effective, and so the Royal Commission recommended that "every train should be provided with sufficient brake-power to stop it absolutely within 500 yards at the highest speed at which it travels, and upon any gradient on the line". Unfortunately the recommendations of the Royal Commission were not mandatory and many railway companies ignored them and carried on with their inadequate braking systems.

An older George Westinghouse photographed in one of his factories. (Tramway and Light Railway Society Archive)

On returning to Britain George Westinghouse agreed

to carry out experiments in braking under the direction of any person appointed by the Institute of Mechanical Engineers. They delegated Captain Douglas Galton, and the experiments became known as the Galton-Westinghouse tests, carried out in 1878. These tests were the first to demonstrate that a sliding wheel was one third as effective when braking than a rolling wheel. They also found that the coefficient of friction increases as the speed falls, that is more braking power is needed at higher speeds. In 1878 he also set up the Westinghouse European Brake Company in France, his first company outside America.

In 1881 the Westinghouse Brake Co. Ltd. was established in London. Up to this point all his brake products had been made in America. Once the English company had been set up, manufacturing gradually transferred to England. However, the aim of the company was always to exploit the Westinghouse patents.

At around this time he turned his attention to another aspect of railway safety, signalling. In 1882 he established the Union Switch and Signal Company. In order to develop a complete electrical and compressed air system he purchased patents, and by 1885 he had gained 38 of them. Later this led to the British brake company being renamed as Westinghouse Brake and Signal Co. Ltd. In 1884 George further expanded by setting up the Westinghouse Brake Company Ltd in Germany.

George Westinghouse had contact with the scientific pioneers of the time. Here he is with Lord Kelvin and Charles Mertz. (Tramway and Light Railway Society Archive)

Another interest of his was the generation of electricity. At this time electrical production was very local and there was no thought of standardisation. Generation was set up on a town by town basis, each with its own specification. So one town may have direct current and the next alternating current. Even where the type of current was the same it was likely that the voltage was different.

In 1885 George Westinghouse purchased a set of

George Westinghouse in his older days advertising his products. At the time the name Westinghouse was synonymous with quality. (Tramway and Light Railway Society Archive)

THE
Westinghouse Electric Company,

LIMITED,

32, VICTORIA STREET, LONDON, S.W.,

AND

32, AVENUE DE L'OPERA, PARIS.

CONTRACTORS FOR

ELECTRIC RAILWAY

AND

TRAMWAY SYSTEMS,

Underground Conduit, Overhead Trolley.

ELECTRIC LOCOMOTIVES

FOR HEAVY TRAFFIC,

The TESLA POLYPHASE ALTERNATING SYSTEM of ELECTRICAL TRANSMISSION, by which POWER INCANDESCENT and ARC LIGHTING may be MOST EFFICIENTLY Operated from the SAME CIRCUITS.

For Full Particulars, Estimates and Pamphlets, apply to the Offices of the Company as above.

An early British advertisement for Westinghouse products. This was before the Trafford Park factory had been built so all purchases were made in America. (Author's collection)

Gaulard-Gibbs transformers and a Siemans AC generator. With these he installed a generation system in Pittsburgh. Typically he set about improving the design of the generator to give a constant voltage and he improved the transformer. By 1886 he had started the Westinghouse Electric Company, with its factory in Pittsburgh (renamed after three years as the Westinghouse Electric and Manufacturing Company) to manufacture AC distribution equipment. He purchased the AC motor patents of Nikola Tesla and developed them for the USA market. By 1889 he had set up 150 AC generating stations powering 300,000 lamps. Such was his association at the time with AC current that it was often referred to by the general public as "Westinghouse Electricity".

By now it was clear that wide spread distribution of electricity was a real possibility, but to do so needed a common system. Edison and GE (the American General Electric Company) favoured DC generation. On the other hand George Westinghouse was firmly an advocate of AC power.

The battle was fierce. The DC camp scored a major publicity advantage (which made the AC interest furious) when in 1889 the Edison Company won the contract to install the electric chair at Sing Sing, New York's State penitentiary. In order to gain an advantage over the AC industry they very publicly chose to wire the chair to an AC current supply (using a standard Westinghouse AC generator). This was done deliberately to discredit Westinghouse and the AC image. By manipulation of the press, the public were informed that AC electricity was more lethal than DC. Death in the electric chair was even called "being Westinghoused". George was furious and refused to sell any AC generators to prison authorities, forcing Edison to make them. George also funded the appeals of the first prisoners sentenced to the electric chair, arguing that it was a cruel and unusual punishment.

By 1890 the Westinghouse empire was prospering. It was estimated that the companies owned by George Westinghouse were worth £12 million with sales in that year of £9 million. However, these figures need to be treated with a little caution as George Westinghouse was rather prone to taking the most favourable view of financial statistics when it came to his companies. Being such a large organisation meant that it was sensitive to the financial state of the USA. In 1891 there was a major downturn and recession, and sales dropped to £5 million with a profit of £200,000, meagre for the vast sum invested in plant and equipment.

However, in 1893 the Westinghouse Company won a major step forward when they were

Brush built car of 1895 for Coventry Corporation, using Westinghouse motors and controllers. (Tramway and Light Railway Society Archive)

chosen to light the World's Columbian Exposition at Chicago. Using Nicola Tesla's AC system of electrical power he could light the exhibition for half the price of Edison's DC system. Edison banned Westinghouse from using his lamps, but George got the contract. In 1895 he built the main works for the Westinghouse Electric and Manufacturing Company in East Pittsburgh. By 1896 Westinghouse and GE had over 75% of the USA electrical market between them. At this time it was believed that electricity would replace steam as the main source of power for railways and George Westinghouse was a major advocate. Another coup for his company was the gaining of the contract to build and install turbines and generators at the Niagara Falls in order to make hydro-electricity. By 1898 he had started the Westinghouse Company Ltd. in St Petersburg, Russia.

In order to be prepared for this and to gain a march

Coventry Corporation tramcar of 1896, rebuilt from a steam tramway trailer, using Westinghouse motors and controllers. (Tramway and Light Railway Society Archive)

Douglas Southern Electric Tramway 1896 tramcar built by Brush and using Westinghouse motors and controllers. (Tramway and Light Railway Society Archive)

over GE, George Westinghouse decided in 1889 to expand his European business into Britain, through the Westinghouse Electric Company, Limited (London). He transferred all the patent rights for the whole world, outside North and South America, from The Westinghouse Electric Company (America) to the London company. The new company did not have a manufacturing factory and all products continued to be made in America, although it did install machinery on contract. In 1899 the British Westinghouse Electric and Manufacturing Company was set up. This was aimed at manufacturing products in England for sale throughout Europe and the Empire. Typical of George Westinghouse, the plan was to establish an enormous factory with vast production capability. He believed this was necessary to meet the demands when electrical power took over from steam as the power source for railways. He considered that vast generating stations would be built near coal mines, and that electrical power would be distributed rather

Glasgow Horse car 994 was the first to be converted to electrical operation in 1899. Westinghouse motors and controllers were fitted and later the tramcar was renumbered 1 to demonstrate it was the first electrically operated tramcar in Glasgow. (Tramway and Light Railway Society Archive)

than carrying coal around the country. If he was right he wanted to have the capability of fulfilling the demand for the new equipment. The initial capital was £1,500,000, a considerable sum in those days. Of this one third was allotted in shares to US Westinghouse in payment for the exclusive rights to Westinghouse electrical patents. Of the remaining £1 million half the shares were purchased by US Westinghouse and the remainder were sold to the public.

However, very soon the urge to expand came again and in 1901 he set up the Societé Anonyme Westinghouse organisation with offices in Paris, and works in Le Havre and Freinville. In the same year the Westinghouse Electricitats-Actiengesellschaft was established in Berlin. In 1903 he looked to other parts of North America and he founded the Canadian Westinghouse Company, Ltd. In 1904 the American Mutoscope & Biograph Co. made silent black and white films of operations in the Westinghouse Pittsburgh Works. The Westinghouse company had a large display in the Louisiana Purchase Exposition held in St Louis that incorporated screenings of the AM&B films, and they also supplied power generators and equipment for the exposition's service plant. However, George was by no means getting all his own way. In 1905, while the Westinghouse Electrical and Manufacturing Company and General Electric of America had over 75% of the electrical market in America, the total sales for GE were $39 million while Westinghouse sold $17 million-worth.

But the bubble was soon to burst. In the summer of 1907, the American economy went through a difficult period, with severe drops in share prices, some businesses going bankrupt and even Wall Street dealers ceasing trading. In October, the Knickerbocker Bank, the Trust Company of America and the Westinghouse Electric Company all went bankrupt. This started what came to be known as the Panic of 1907 when hundreds of banks failed. Whether as a result of over extending himself or because of his tendency to creative accounting is not sure, but George Westinghouse lost control of all his companies, though he still maintained a directorship in many of them. In an attempt to save George, Nikola Tesla sold his AC electrical patents to the Westinghouse company for a nominal sum. However, while the company survived, this did not save George, and later led to financial ruin for Tesla himself. By 1911 George's type of entrepreneurial style was out of favour and he was forced to sever all ties with every one of his companies. Possibly this was the result of shareholders venting their feelings for years of poor or non-existent dividends. This must have been a bitter blow for him and probably contributed to his decline in health. He died on 12 March 1914 aged 67. As a Civil War Veteran he was buried in Arlington National Cemetery. At his death his wife of 47 years, Marguerite, said that she had nothing to live for anymore and she died three months later on 23 June. She was buried with George at Arlington National Cemetery. In 1930, a memorial to George Westinghouse, funded by his employees, was placed in Schenley Park in Pittsburgh.

In 1899 St Helen's & District Tramway ordered 20 bogie tramcars (numbers 17 – 36) from the just formed British Westinghouse Company, who sub-contracted the body building to Brush. The motors and controllers were provided by Westinghouse. (Tramway and Light Railway Society Archive)

Plymouth Corporation ordered six tramcars from Milnes to open their electric tramway, converted from a company horse tramway. The first six trams had Westinghouse electrical equipment. (Tramway and Light Railway Society Archive)

During his lifetime George Westinghouse had taken out around 400 patents and established 86 companies in nine different countries, detailed in Appendix 1. But his most enduring legacy is raising the level of passenger safety on the world's railways with his braking system and the signalling and track circuitry innovations. These are still in use today, more than a century after his invention.

When Norwich Electric Tramways opened their electric tramway in 1900 they used Brush built trams with Westinghouse electrical equipment. (Tramway and Light Railway Society Archive)

Chapter 2
THE DEVELOPMENT OF BRITISH WESTINGHOUSE ELECTRIC AND MANUFACTURING COMPANY

The Westinghouse Electric Company, Limited (London) had been established in 1889 to promote and sell Westinghouse products in Britain, Europe and the Empire. This company was distinct from the Westinghouse European Brake Company and the Westinghouse Brake Company Limited, which had been set up to exploit the railway braking business. The Westinghouse Electric Company, Limited (London) was directed at the expanding field of electrical production, distribution and use. It did not manufacture anything, all products being imported from America.

However, the dream of George Westinghouse was that electricity would become the major power source

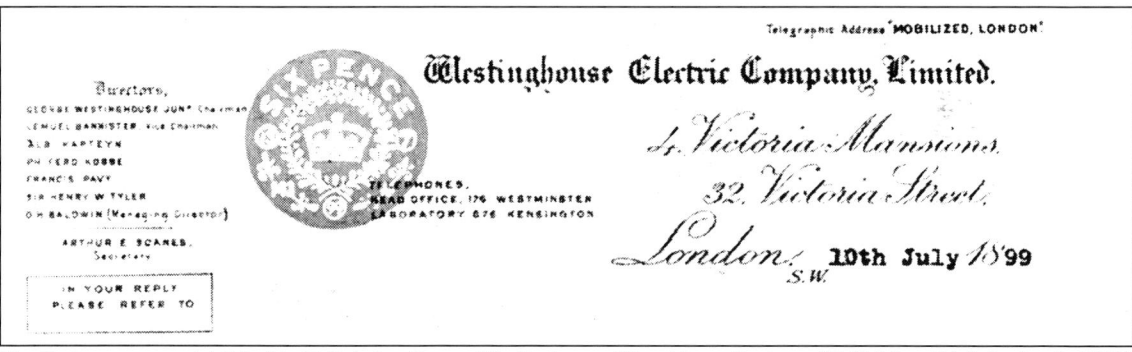

The first company established in Britain by George Westinghouse did not have the term "British" as this letterhead of 1899 shows. (Author's collection)

The Westinghouse exhibit at the tramways exhibition held in 1900 in London, showing the tram demonstrating its prowess by carrying plenty of guests. (Tramway and Light Railway Society Archive)

This photograph of the 1900 exhibition clearly shows the conduit system, chosen by Westinghouse to impress the LCC. (Tramway and Light Railway Society Archive)

for all industrial, transport and home consumption. In particular he had a vision that most if not all the railways in Europe would be powered by electricity. In America it had been shown that for suburban railways electricity was the most effective power source. He considered that Britain was so densely populated it was virtually all suburban. He predicted that the future would bring a system where electrical generation would be carried out near coal fields, and instead of transporting vast quantities of coal, electricity would be distributed instantly through wires. All this would need enormous quantities of new mechanical equipment, most of which his companies were expert at producing. So he wanted to be in a position to be able to fulfil the demand, particularly if that meant beating General Electric.

His plan was to build a factory in England large enough to meet the enormous demands he expected. So in 1899 he set up the British Westinghouse Electric and Manufacturing Company. There is no doubt that he quite deliberately used the word British in the title in order to minimise the anti-American attitudes that he had met when visiting Britain. The initial capital of the company was £1.5 million, a very substantial sum in those days. Of this £500,000 was allotted in ordinary shares to the American Westinghouse Company in payment for exclusive rights on its electrical patents (which begs the question of what happened to the arrangement with the Westinghouse Electric Company, Limited (London), which was still in existence). Cash of £1 million was to be raised by an issue of 6 per cent preference shares. The Board of the company first met on 10 July 1899 with George Westinghouse as Chairman. Over the following days he signed an agreement to purchase land for the factory. This was 130 acres on the Trafford Park Estate in Manchester.

The Trafford Park had been the home of Sir Humphrey de Trafford. In 1761 the Bridgewater canal was opened and this formed the southern boundary to

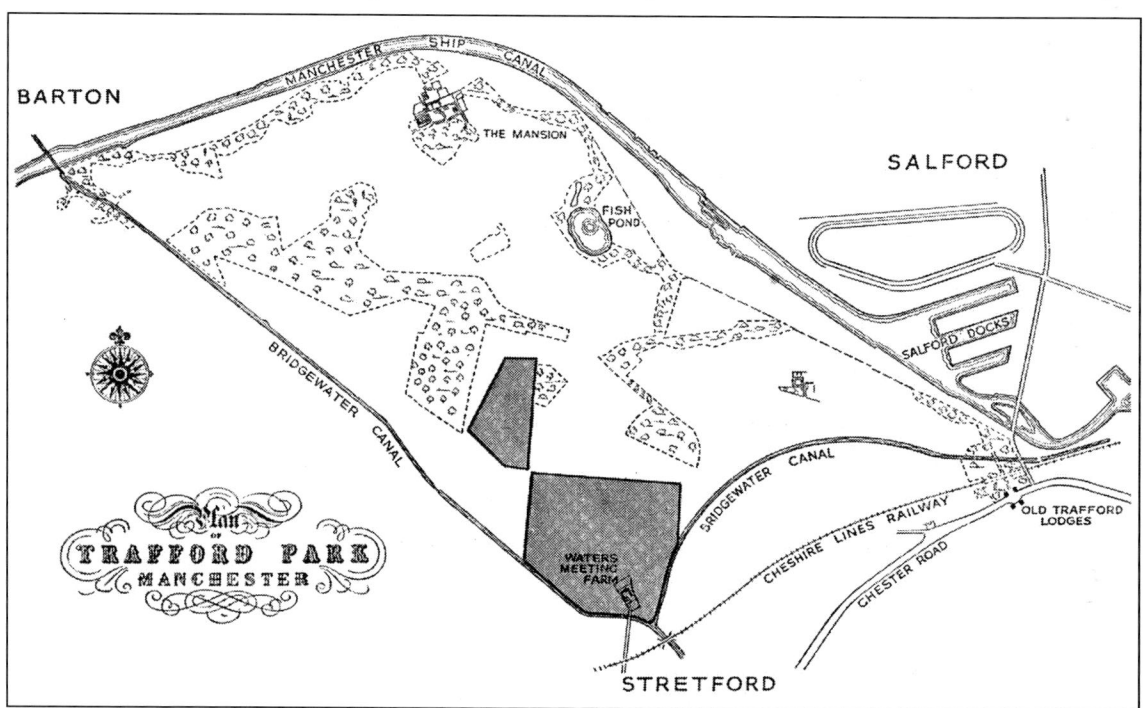

Trafford Park in 1899 showing the sites purchased by George Westinghouse. (Author's collection)

the park. In 1887 work started on the massive Manchester Ship Canal, which followed the course of the River Irwell around Trafford Park. Effectively the park became an island and Trafford Hall was the only residence. Sir Humphrey de Trafford decided to dispose of the property and the 1,200 acres of park. It was purchased in 1896 by Mr E.T. Hooley, a financier. For a while the future of the park was under debate, the main contenders being a racecourse and/or residential housing. However, M. Stevens, General Manager of the Ship Canal, was seeking more shipping trade. He approached Mr Hooley and suggested using the land for new factories. Mr Hooley agreed.

Trafford Park was the estate for Trafford Hall. (Author's collection)

Railway links with the main railway companies via the Cheshire Lines Railway were set up, and the land was advertised for sale. In 1899 the new British Westinghouse Company purchased 100 acres on the southernmost portion, bounded on two sides by the Bridgewater canal, with another 30-acre plot close by. The location was also close to the Cheshire Lines Railway link, giving two major transport facilities.

Having such ambitious plans meant that it would take time to set up the manufacturing factory. In the meantime products made in America could be sold by the British company. In typical extravagant style George Westinghouse exhibited at the first Tramways and Light Railways Exhibition. This was held in London in 1900. All the major tram manufacturing concerns were represented. Large stands were erected with complete tramcars and all the thousands of parts and accessories needed by tramway systems. However, Westinghouse was not content with an ordinary stand. He had a 310-foot long tramway erected in the hall and ran an open top bogie car made by G.F. Milnes. In an astute move he used the conduit system of power supply, knowing that this was the favoured system for the proposed London County Council electric tramway. No doubt the managers and engineers from the various tramway systems were given full demonstrations of the power of the motors and the effectiveness of the brakes. After the exhibition, Westinghouse was able to sell the whole tramway, and a gas engine and dynamo, to London County Council. The LCC paid £900 for the tramcar, £175 for the rails and conduit, and £75 for the engine and dynamo. It was said at the time that the payment for the track only covered the removal of the rails and conduit. British Westinghouse felt that by getting their conduit in first they would be in a better position when the specifica-

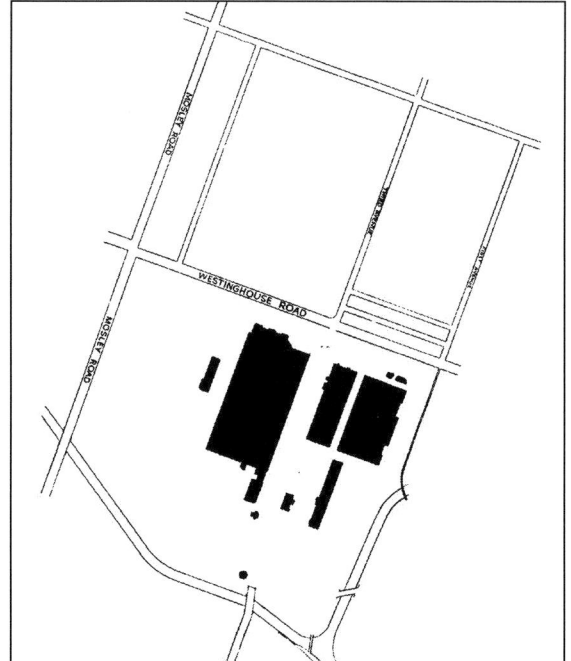

Plan of the factory in the early1900s. (Tramway and Light Railway Society Archive)

Part of the Canadian workforce brought over by James Stewart (front row right) to improve the speed of building. (Tramway and Light Railway Society Archive)

James Stewart (in light suit behind the seated figure) and the American workforce. (Tramway and Light Railway Society Archive)

The scale of the construction can be seen from the amount of materials being brought in and the skeleton frameworks in the background. (Author's collection)

Westinghouse products, work was proceeding at a pace on the new factory. Interestingly tenders for the steel construction work that formed the frame for each building were sent to American firms as well as British. While the American firms quoted a shorter delivery time, by as much as five months, the contract was awarded to Messrs Dorman, Long and Co. of Middlesbrough. However, the woodwork for the flooring of the buildings was purchased from America. George Westinghouse had decided that the orders coming in from British customers warranted production in the new Trafford Park factory to begin in 1901, just eighteen months from the purchase of the land. George Westinghouse also had plans to house his workers near to the factory. The Trafford Park Estates Company had set up a separate firm "Trafford Park Dwellings Company" to erect and rent housing for families working in factories in the Park. Westinghouse arranged with the Dwellings Company that it should build the accommodation, so significant numbers of terraced houses were built not far from the Westinghouse works. It was reported that the houses had electricity for lighting and gas for heating and their own water supply. The idea was that by providing comfortable dwellings,

tion was determined and the tenders let. The LCC transferred the line to Camberwell tramway depot where it was used by the Tramways Committee to prepare specifications for their new electric tramway. Members of local Authorities were invited to inspect the trial line in an attempt to win their approval for the new tramway. As it turned out British Westinghouse missed out on the track contract because competitors quoted lower prices.

In 1901 the exhibition was repeated in Glasgow, where the large Westinghouse stand was housed in its own separate building. In 1902 the exhibition returned to London and again another 310-foot long tramway was erected and potential buyers given rides along it on tramcar number 1 of the Tyneside Tramways and Tramroads Company. This time the power supply was by overhead running wire, with ornate traction poles. By 1902 it was clear that, apart from a few odd exceptions, tramways would be using overhead power supply.

While these exhibitions were promoting

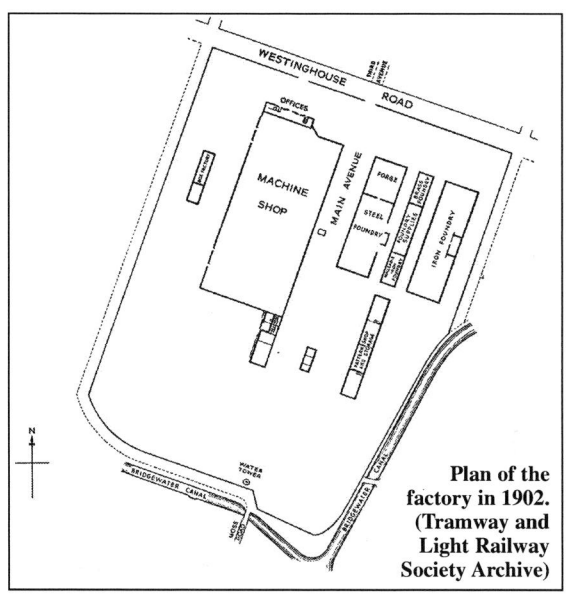

Plan of the factory in 1902. (Tramway and Light Railway Society Archive)

in contrast to many in Manchester, a high class of labour would be attracted to work in the factory.

By the end of the first year just the foundations had been laid and local contractors were saying that it would take a further five years for the factory to be completed. The first annual general meeting of the company was about to take place and rumours were going around that work on the factory had been abandoned. At the AGM, held on 23 November 1900 and presided over by Hon. R. Clerc Parsons (Chairman of the Executive Committee) there were more problems than just the delay of the factory. A gloss was put on the delays by saying that work was being pushed forward as rapidly as possible. Explanations also had to be made about a row between British Westinghouse and the Metropolitan Railway. The latter had invited tenders for the conversion of their underground lines to electric power. British Westinghouse had put forward a tender, but had also applied to Parliament for powers to carry out the conversion. The Metropolitan Railway was furious, it preferred

The factory under construction. (Author's collection)

Construction continues. (Author's collection)

A temporary overhead crane is used to lift roof trusses. (Author's collection)

Construction continued at a much faster pace. (Author's collection)

The interior of the machine shop nears completion. (Author's collection)

Raising the giant overhead cranes. (Author's collection)

the tender of another company and rushed to protest that British Westinghouse had taken the action without either discussing the matter with them or obtaining the company's consent. At the AGM the Hon. Clerc Parsons said that parliamentary approval was a necessary part of the tender process (though without mentioning that none of the other eight tendering companies felt the same need). No doubt this brash approach to business did little to endear the American Company to the British establishment.

George Westinghouse was concerned at the delays in building the factory and, rejecting the slow pace of the local contractors, turned to his home country. He found James C. Stewart, a Canadian-born building contractor, who said he would complete the job in fifteen months from 1 January 1901. In reality he beat his estimate by finishing the job in less than a year. The scale of this endeavour was enormous. The nine factory buildings covered 30 acres of the site. The largest building of the complex was the Machine Shop. It had five aisles each nearly 900 feet long. The combined width was 400 feet and the main aisles had a clearance height of 60 feet and an overall height of 82 feet. Five railway lines ran inside the length of the factory. The floor area was divided into specialist areas such as turbine blade manufacture, the turbine test area, the main large electrical aisle, industrial motors and a motor test area. At the front of the Machine Shop were the offices. These were contained within a purpose-built six-storey building. The next largest building was the Iron Foundry. Nearly 600 feet long, over 300 feet wide and over 60 feet high, it was able to cast everything from small components to castings weighing many tons. It had six main smelting cupolas, the total capacity being 46 tons of iron per hour. The molten metal was poured into ladles of between 10 tons and 25 tons capacity moved by cranes, with hand-carried ladles for smaller work.

Installing the vast number of machines that would be required to manufacture the products. (Author's collection)

There was a Brass Foundry contained within the Iron Foundry. This was able to make items from ¼-ounce to 30cwt. There were smaller buildings containing the transformer shop, forge, many and various stores, a box factory for packing items, a works canteen and the research department for the development of products. The total area of land covered by roofing was 40 acres (over the years additional buildings were constructed and by the 1930s no less than 56 acres were roofed over). Altogether the factory buildings took 11 million bricks, 10 million feet of timber and 16,000 tons of steel. Some 4,000 workers were employed in the construction. Within the factory site as a whole there were 16 miles of railway tracks of which

Aerial photograph of the completed factory before the days of clean air legislation. (Tramway and Light Railway Society Archive)

The water tower became a well known feature of the Westinghouse site. It had to be removed in the 2nd World War as it was felt it would be a landmark for enemy bombers. (Tramway and Light Railway Society Archive)

The Foundation Stone with the list of eminent people involved in its laying. (Tramway and Light Railway Society Archive)

10 miles was on the standard gauge, the remainder being narrow gauge using Westinghouse electric locomotives. On top of this the works also had land on which it built a village to house its workers. When the works opened it employed around 3,000 men. At its height this had expanded to around 13,000 employees. Indeed the impression that is given when looking at old photos of the inside of the various shops is a hive of activity that was extremely labour intensive. An impression of the numbers involved is given by the photographs of the workers leaving the factory at the end of their shift. To keep the factory supplied with water it had its own water tower – an elaborate cast iron structure over 200 feet high with a capacity of 223 tons of water. It became a landmark for the factory, instantly recognisable. Indeed it was such a feature that the government ordered its demolition during the early years of the Second World War. It was feared that German pilots would use it to navigate themselves around Manchester.

It was reported that James Stewart raised the productivity of the British workers considerably by changing the practices of the day. These included replacing the old hand riveting techniques used for the framework of the building with mechanical tools. With the millions of bricks to be laid the old system of using manual hod carriers was replaced with steam hoists, able to keep the bricklayers supplied with vast quantities of bricks. The output of the bricklayers was increased from 500 bricks per day to as much as 2,500 on a straight run. However the raising in efficiency was not without some consequences. In November 1901 400 joiners went on strike because their hour lunch break was being cut back and they felt they would not have sufficient time to digest their lunches. This was seized on by the technical press who supported the actions of the joiners against these new American practices, much preferring their traditional British ways.

On a more favourable note the site was visited by the Lord Mayors of London and Manchester on 3rd

The ceremony of laying the Foundation Stone. (Tramway and Light Railway Society Archive)

August 1901 in order to lay the Foundation Stone. It is typical of the publicity-minded George Westinghouse that this was used as the excuse for a large ceremony. The Foundation Stone probably holds the record for having the most number of dignitaries laying it. The stone is inscribed "This Foundation Stone was Laid by The Right Honourable The Lord Mayor of London Alderman Frank Green assisted by The Right Honourable The Lord Mayor of Manchester Thomas Briggs JP and W Vaughan Morgan Alderman, Joseph Lawrence MP, Freemen of the City

The factory opened and ready for production. (Author's collection)

The "Holy Forty" in America. (Author's collection)

of London, George Westinghouse Chairman". In the event George himself was ill and unable to attend so the Deputy Chairman, Mr C. W. Benson hosted on behalf of the company. It was not long before the factory was fitted out with all the latest machine tools from America. The machines in the factory were brought to Manchester by railway. Rather than tranship the thousands of items, rails were laid directly into the buildings and the machine parts unloaded exactly where they were needed. One lathe was so large it took twenty five trucks to bring it to the works.

George Westinghouse had realised that he would need well trained workers and he intended

A Westinghouse narrow gauge battery locomotive of the type used in the Trafford Park works, this photo is of the same type of locomotive used in the American factory. (Author's collection)

This photograph of the iron foundry showing just how labour intensive manufacturing was at that time. (Author's collection)

Some of the housing of the Trafford Park "village" built to house Westinghouse workers. (Author's collection)

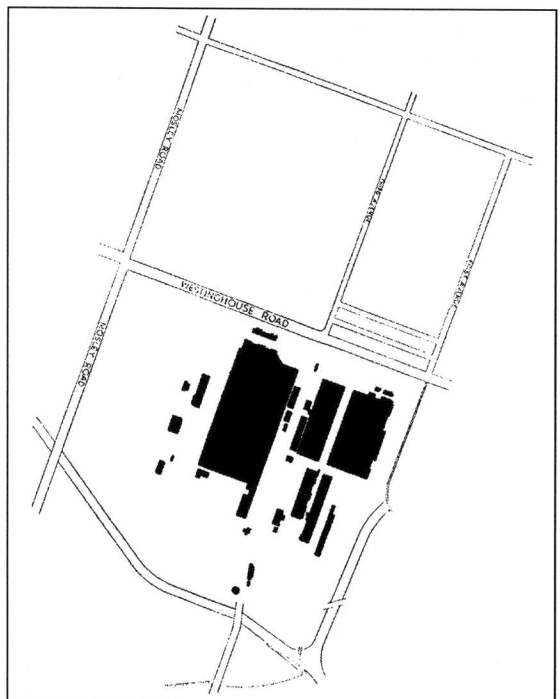

The plan of the factory in the 1910s showing the expansion in the first decade. (Tramway and Light Railway Society Archive)

that they should use American methods. So in 1899 he selected a group of workers who, at their own expense, travelled to his factory in Pittsburgh. They each had to sign a contract where they would remain with the American Company for 5,480 working hours at 20-25 cents an hour and, on return, to remain with the British Company at a salary of £150-£175 per annum. So it may well have been that the company purchased the tickets and then deducted the cost over a period of time while they worked in America, as few could have afforded the cost of a journey to the USA. They spent two to three years in the American factory and then in 1902 returned to Manchester to form the nucleus of the workforce. This group acquired the name "The Holy Forty". Quite why this was is lost in the mists of time. There is no record of how many travelled to America, though all the sources agree that it was not forty! So we must assume that around forty returned to work in the new factory. It can only be guessed that the tag "Holy" came about from the knowledge of operating the American machinery, suffice to say that an alternative name for them was soon found, the Forty Thieves. However, whilst in America they were known as the "British Specials".

While in America one group stayed at a boarding house that was near a laundry, with a siren that was sounded at 7.00am every morning – they called it 'Hooter Hell'. George Westinghouse always prided himself on the relationship he had with his workers. However, it is clear that the American way of working was very much at odds with the British ways. One facility in the offices that must have seemed strange to most British workers, was the placing of spittoons that the Americans (and the Holy Forty) made copious use of. Some innovations were soon dropped, such as the use of an internal police force to patrol the shops to see that everyone was working. The workers also strongly objected to using American standard screw threads, insisting on British standards. These were changed, though it was also due to resistance from customers to anything that was not made to British standards. In fact it is difficult to get a good feeling for life in the factory. All the records are the official statements which either always put a glowing picture, or just concentrate on the financial affairs. However, there is a hint in the autobiography of Norman Swindin, a chemical engineer who had no connection with British Westinghouse. Mr Swindin, in the early 1900s, lodged in Manchester

Plan of the factory in the 1920s. (Tramway and Light Railway Society Archive)

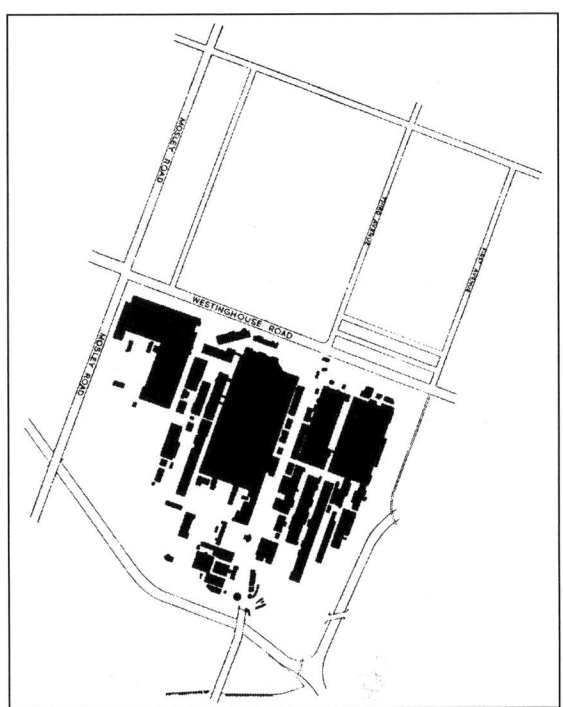

Plan of the factory in the 1930s. (Tramway and Light Railway Society Archive)

sharing with three clerks working at the new British Westinghouse factory. Mr Swindin writes that hiring and firing at the Trafford Park factory was so frequent that a steady job was rare indeed. If you saw an elderly man with a beard he would in all probability be an apprentice, and that any youngster you might see would in all likelihood be a foreman or chargehand. It was also said that a first manager, Baron von Trube, had an autocratic manner with a lurid vocabulary. One of the clerks lodging with Mr Swindin was von Trube's

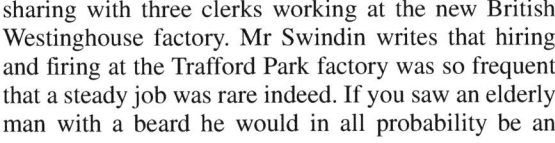

The machine shop fully fitted out. (Author's collection)

The end of the day sees hundreds of workers leaving the factory for home. (Author's collection)

private secretary. One of his tasks was to help the Baron in the English way of life. Apparently on one occasion the Baron had been invited to a Burns dinner and instructed his Secretary that he wanted to appear to be knowledgeable about the works of Burns. Mr Swindin advised the secretary to borrow "A Garland of Sweet Scented Flowers" from the library, that had the original version of "Coming Through the Rye". The Baron appeared at the dinner and recited the poem in its original form. As his grasp of English was not perfect he was unaware that the poem rejoiced in illicit open air love making, However, his audience were

Workers outside the factory, probably at lunchtime, with the tram service behind them. (Tramway and Light Railway Society Archive)

very aware and he made a great impression (that the Baron put down to the skill of his recitation).

Von Trube was not the only character at the works. The first Works Superintendent W.C. Mitchell used to arrive at the works in his own gig with cockaded footman. At the time Moss Road, the approach to the works, was quite narrow so he would send an advance guard to clear the road of pedestrians so as not to slow his gig. He was also very critical of the Manchester weather. Pointing to a tower on the hills to the north, he would say that if you could not see the tower, it was because it was raining and if you could see it then it was about to rain.

In the first year there were some notable successes. Two 1,000 horse power generating engines were delivered to King Edward VII at Sandringham. Arc lights were provided for Selfridges store in Oxford Street, and eight massive generators for the Lots Road Power Station of the Metropolitan and District Railway. In 1903 British Westinghouse won the contracts for 100 bogie cars and 100 four wheel cars for London County Council. This order was a repeat of the first 200 tramcars for the opening of the electric tramway. However, British Westinghouse was not successful for that first order. At this time it was the practice to publish the list of all contractors and their quotes at the time the winner was announced. The first 200 tramcars cost £119, 440 and the contractor was Dick, Kerr and Co. The Westinghouse quote for the second 200 was £118,880, the lowest of all the quotes (this time Dick, Kerr and Co quoted £125,868). So it may be that British Westinghouse, armed with the first quotes, deliberately put a low price in so that they could put the substantial amount of work into the new factory.

But the rush to electrical power forecast by George Westinghouse failed to materialise. Indeed in Britain there were a total of around 20,000 electric tramcars built for use on all the tramway systems in the British Isles. In the period between 1883 and 1905 (22 years) roughly half this total had been put in service. The other half were built between 1906 and 1953 (47 years). The peak period of production was between 1895 and 1905 when the big city tramway systems were both converting to electrical operation and expanding their networks. In this respect British Westinghouse were a little late on the scene.

British Westinghouse did gain the contract for the electrification of the Mersey Railway, but this was not enough to use the capacity of the factory. The Directors continued to be bullish at the Annual General Meetings, promising that tomorrow would bring better days. However, by 1904 it was clear there were distinct problems. The overall profit carried forward was £2,809 and no payment was made to debenture shareholders. Indeed the meagre profit was only achieved by some creative accounting. Shareholders were not at all pleased, and the Financial News added insult to injury by asserting that the Westinghouse Annual Report was written in a language that was not English, but that resembled it sufficiently to be judged American! Matters deteriorated with a loss of £15,407 declared the following year, 1905. In America the parent company was losing ground to General Electric. 1906 saw another loss and George Westinghouse brought in Newcomb Carlton, an American "Strong Man", to take the British company in hand. Executive management was trimmed and unused parts of the site sold off. In 1905 a letter was sent to staff "prohibiting tea-drinking between meal-times for lady stenographers and lady clerks, except when medical certificates warrant it." Things started to get better in 1907, though a downturn in trade did not help. The value of the company was written down from £3,250,000 to £1,875,000, by revaluing the £5 shares to £3 and £10 shares to £5, taking off roughly half the value from shareholders. Then in October an almost fatal blow was struck. The American parent company, Westinghouse Electric and Manufacturing Company, went into receivership. It was touch and go whether this would pull down the British company. It meant that Newcomb Carlton had to seek £300,000 from the City of London to pay off debts. He succeeded, but had to allow the stockbrokers power to appoint the majority of the board. George Westinghouse retained the title of Chairman, but he had lost control of his company. It was clear that his precarious financial accounting had led to a loss of faith in the company. New York merchant bankers saved the American company and while George Westinghouse stayed as President the executive power went to a banker's appointee.

1908 saw a pick-up in business with the first use of

Aerial photograph of the factory site at its fullest extent. (Author's collection)

6,000 volt single phase AC supply on the Thamshavn-Lokken metre-gauge railway in Norway. The end of the year saw another loss, but all loans had been paid off giving a far more improved financial position. At the end of 1909 the company roughly broke even and then showed a profit in 1910. However, these years were not smooth ones for the board. They were having difficulties with George Westinghouse. In 1909 the board voted him out of the chairman post, replacing him with John Annan Bryce. Then in 1910 things had reached such a peak that he was voted off the board entirely. The American company still owned half the British company, but George no longer had any power in the American company and so could not resist the indignity of being dismissed from the company he set up.

However, the British company continued to prosper. In 1913 profits exceeded £100,000 for the first time. The start of the First World War in 1914 saw the factory turning to munitions work. George Westinghouse died on 12 March, having been parted from the British company for four years.

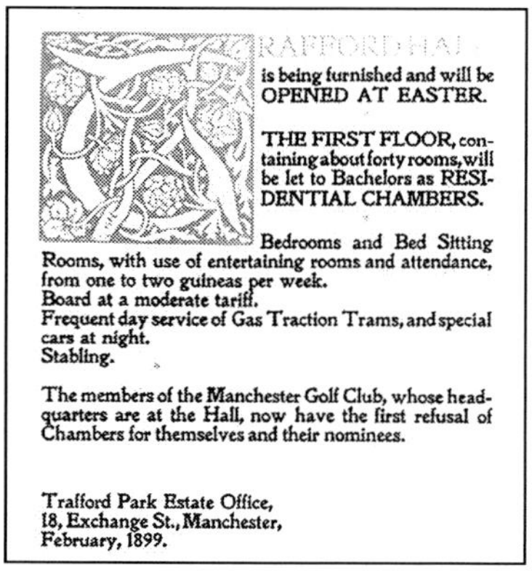
is being furnished and will be OPENED AT EASTER.

THE FIRST FLOOR, containing about forty rooms, will be let to Bachelors as RESIDENTIAL CHAMBERS.

Bedrooms and Bed Sitting Rooms, with use of entertaining rooms and attendance, from one to two guineas per week.
Board at a moderate tariff.
Frequent day service of Gas Traction Trams, and special cars at night.
Stabling.

The members of the Manchester Golf Club, whose headquarters are at the Hall, now have the first refusal of Chambers for themselves and their nominees.

Trafford Park Estate Office,
18, Exchange St., Manchester,
February, 1899.

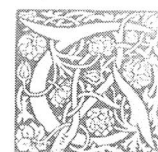

The original Hall building was refurbished and the first floor converted to what today would be called executive apartments. (Author's collection)

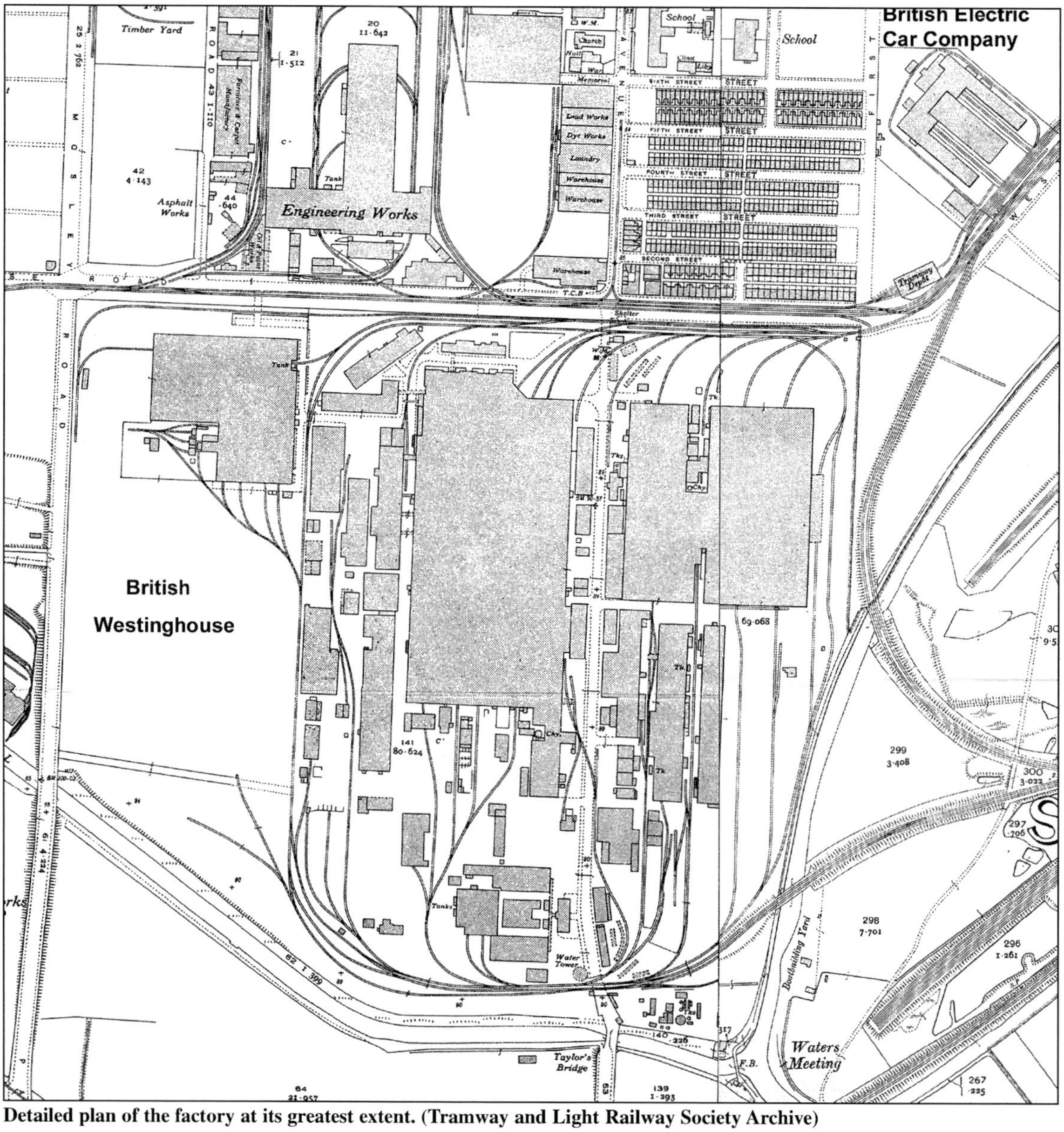

Detailed plan of the factory at its greatest extent. (Tramway and Light Railway Society Archive)

Chapter 3

THE TRAMWAY PRODUCTS OF BRITISH WESTINGHOUSE AND METROVICK

British Westinghouse was an electrical manufacturer, producing a wide range of medium and heavy electrical engineering products. The Trafford Park Factory included separate iron and brass foundries, a large forge and machine shop. The tramway products were somewhat of a sideline for the factory. The products for tramways occupied a relatively small area of the complex. The major tramway products fell into three areas:

CONTROLLERS
MOTORS
ELECTRO-MAGNETIC BRAKES

In addition there was a range of the smaller electrical items required to fully fit out the electrical side of a tramcar. These included canopy switches, breakers and lightning arresters. Finally the factory produced their most unusual tramcars for the army in World War I.

FIRST WORLD WAR TRAMCARS

This specialising on the purely electrical equipment led to an immediate difficulty when it came to gaining orders. When a tramway undertaking asked for tenders for new tramcars they wanted complete trams, not separate bodies and electrical equipment. There were four options open to British Westinghouse:

1. To hope that the purchaser would specify Westinghouse electrical equipment.
2. To hope that tram body manufacturers would choose their electrical products.
3. To officially link with a tram body manufacturer to offer a complete package.
4. To bid themselves for the order and then sub-contract the body to a tramcar builder.

The first three options would have restricted the control of tendering by British Westinghouse, so they chose the fourth path. They put quotations for business in their own right. In the early days, around the 1900s, it was the practice for tramway undertakings to publish details of all the tenders that they had received. It is informative to examine one in detail. This comes from the pages of the Tramway and Railway World for April 1903, and refers to the successful tender by British Westinghouse for the 100 bogie and 100 four-wheel tramcars for the second phase of the London County

The first tramcar sold by Westinghouse to the LCC was the tram used at the 1900 exhibition. It eventually became number 101 in the LCC fleet. Later it was cut down to single deck and renumbered 110. (Tramway and Light Railway Society Archive)

Westinghouse won the contract to build one hundred four wheel tramcars for the London County Council, classified as Class C numbered 202 – 301. (Tramway and Light Railway Society Archive)

Another of the Class C tramcars, with Brush bodies. The other tram is either a Class A or a Class D. (Tramway and Light Railway Society Archive)

Council Tramways. The two tables are shown on the following pages. This was by any standards an exceptional order. Even at the height of the tramway building boom an order for 200 tramcars would have been extremely attractive. In the early 1900s, when the boom was on the wane, the conversion by the LCC to electrical operation came as a major boost to the tramway manufacturing industry.

It was evident that the London County Council would be purchasing large numbers of tramcars in order to run the electric tramway they were building.

The tender attracted plenty of interest, with 10 companies making 25 bids for the bogie contract and 32 bids for the single truck contract. The listing clearly shows the amount of mixing and matching that the tendering firms were willing to do to meet the wishes of the LCC. The first contracts for the initial 200 tramcars had gone to Dick, Kerr & Co. with Brill bogies or trucks, ERTCW bodies and, naturally, Dick, Kerr & Co. electrical equipment, at a cost of £119,440. Often tramway organisations would purchase their following orders from the same company that supplied the first tramcars. The reasons for this is that the maintenance engineers can get a better understanding of the characteristics of particular manufacturer's items, fewer varieties of spares are required, and in extreme situations parts can be cannibalised off other cars. So it is likely that Dick, Kerr & Co felt confident about securing this second order. However, there seems to be an over-riding principle of the LCC Tramways Committee to choose the lowest tender. In this case British

The contract for the next 100 tramcars numbered 302 – 401, Class D, was also won by Westinghouse. (Tramway and Light Railway Society Archive)

75 of the Class D tramcars had bodies built by Brush, the remaining 25 were bodied by the British Electric Car Company. This car was built by Brush. (Tramway and Light Railway Society Archive)

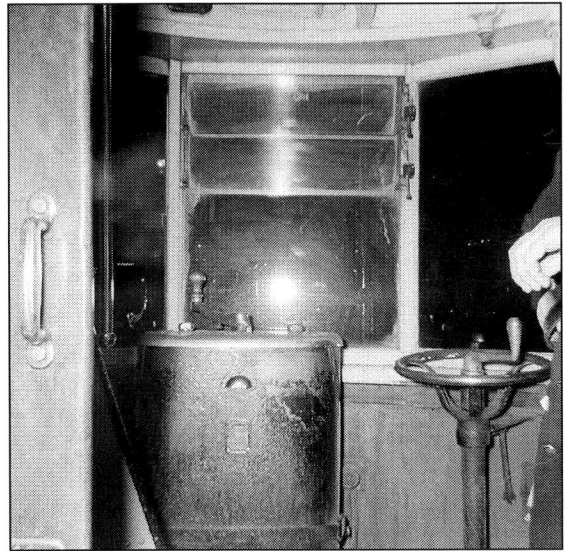

Westinghouse controller in a London tramcar. (Tramway and Light Railway Society Archive)

Westinghouse motor fitted to a wheel-set. (Author's collection)

A Westinghouse controller opened for repair. (Tramway and Light Railway Society Archive)

Westinghouse track brake. (Author's collection)

List of tenders received by the London County Council for bogie cars

No	Name of Firm	Price for 100 cars £	Names of proposed sub-contractors				Delivery	
			Truck	Body	Plough	Electrical Equipment	1st 50 Wks	2nd 50 Wks
1	British Westinghouse	65,968	McGuire	Brush	A. Reyrolle	Own	22	28
2	British Westinghouse	66,696	Brill	Brush	A. Reyrolle	Own	22	28
3	British Westinghouse	67,568	McGuire	Milnes	A. Reyrolle	Own	22	28
4	British Westinghouse	68,368	Brill	Milnes	A. Reyrolle	Own	22	28
5	Dick, Kerr & Co.	69,364	Own	ERTCW	J. G. White	Own	24	24
6	Dick, Kerr & Co..	69,864	Brill	ERTCW	J. G. White	Own	24	24
7	BTH	69,896	Brush	Brush	J. G. White	Own	20	25
8	Brush	70,180	Own	Own	J. G. White	Own	18	26
9	MTH	70,396	McGuire	Brush	J. G. White	Own	20	25
10	Witting Bros.	71,046	McGuire	Brush	J. G .White	Own	26	26
11	BTH	71,196	Brill	Brush	J. G. White	Own	20	25
12	Siemens & Halske	71,226	Brill	Milnes	--	Own	20	20
13	Witting Bros.	72,046	Brill	Brush	J. G. White	Own	26	36
14	British Schuckert	72,278	Brush	Brush	J. G. White	Own	21	27
15	Hungarian Rly.	72,374	Own	Own	--	Siemens	48	65
16	Brush	72,380	Brill	Own	J. G. White	Own	18	26
17	Electrical Co.	72,458	Brush	Brush	J. G. White	Own	26	32
18	Siemens & Halske	72,526	Milnes	Milnes	--	Own	20	20
19	Hurst, Nelson & Co.	72,774	Own	Own	J. G. White	Witting	35	47
20	Hungarian Rly	72,774	Brill	Own	--	Siemens	48	65
21	British Schuckert	72,790	McGuire	Brush	J. G. White	Own	21	27
22	Electrical Co.	73,558	Milnes	Milnes	J. G. White	Own	26	32
23	Electrical Co.	73,804	Brill	Brush	J. G. White	Own	26	32
24	Electrical Co.	73,984	Brill	Milnes	J. G. White	Own	26	32
25	Hurst, Nelson & Co.	75,974	Brill	Own	J. G. White	Witting	35	47

Another early customer was London United Tramways. (Tramway and Light Railway Society Archive)

Westinghouse undercut the Dick, Kerr quote by around £8,000, a handsome saving in 1903. The second batch of 200 tramcars was purchased at a slightly lower cost than the first batch.

It seems that British Westinghouse was very unsure what the LCC were after. It put in four separate tenders for the bogie cars and six for the four-wheel cars. All obviously had Westinghouse electrical equipment, while the tenders gave a choice between McGuire or Brill bogies and trucks and bodies by Brush, Milnes or British Electric Car Co. The London County Council Tramways Committee chose the least expen-

List of tenders received by the London County Council for single truck cars

No	Name of Firm	Price for 100 cars £	Truck	Body	Plough	Electrical Equipment	Delivery 1st 50 Wks	Delivery 2nd 50 Wks
1	British Westinghouse	52,912	McGuire	Brush	A. Reyrolle	Own	22	28
2	British Westinghouse	53,012	Brill	Brush	A. Reyrolle	Own	22	28
3	British Westinghouse	53,912	McGuire	British Electric Car Co.	A. Reyrolle	Own	22	28
4	British Westinghouse	54,012	Brill	British Electric Car Co.	A. Reyrolle	Own	22	28
5	Brush	55,370	Own	Own	J. G. White	Own	18	26
6	British Westinghouse	55,712	McGuire	Milnes	A. Reyrolle	Own	22	28
7	British Westinghouse	55,812	Brill	Milnes	A. Reyrolle	Own	22	28
8	Brush	56,470	Brill	Own	J. G. White	Own	18	26
9	Dick, Kerr & Co.	56,504	Own	ERTCW	J. G. White	Own	24	24
10	BTH	56,766	Brush	Brush	J. G. White	Own	20	25
11	Dick, Kerr & Co.	56,904	Brill	ERTCW	J. G. White	Own	24	24
12	Witting Bros.	56,924	McGuire	Brush	J. G. White	Own	26	26
13	BTH	56,966	McGuire	Brush	J. G. White	Own	20	25
14	BTH	57,116	Brill	Brush	J. G. White	Own	20	25
15	Witting Bros.	57,224	Brill	Brush	J. G. White	Own	21	27
16	British Schuckert	57,644	Brush	Brush	J. G. White	Own	21	25
17	BTH	57,716	Brush	British Electric Car Co.	J. G. White	Own	20	25
18	British Schuckert	57,844	McGuire	Brush	J. G. White	Own	21	27
19	BTH	57,916	McGuire	BEC	J. G. White	Own	20	25
20	Siemens & Halske	58,025	Milnes	Milnes	--	Own	20	20
21	BTH	58,066	Brill	BEC	J. G. White	Own	20	25
22	BTH	58,266	Brush	Milnes	J. G. White	Own	20	25
23	BTH	58,466	McGuire	Milnes	J. G. White	Own	20	25
24	Hungarian Rly.	58,495	Own	Own	--	Siemens	48	65
25	BTH	58,616	Brill	Milnes	J. G. White	Own	20	25
26	Electrical Co.	59,142	Brill	Brush	J. G. White	Own	26	32
27	Electrical Co.	59,272	Brush	Brush	J. G. White	Own	26	32
28	Hungarian Rly	59,495	Brill	Own	--	Siemens	48	65
29	Electrical Co.	60,314	Milnes	Milnes	J. G. White	Own	26	32
30	Electrical Co.	60,592	Brill	Milnes	J. G. White	German	26	32
31	Hurst, Nelson & Co.	61,715	Own	Own	J. G. White	Own	35	47
32	Hurst, Nelson & Co.	62,515	Brill	Own	J. G. White	Own	35	47

sive tender, which was from British Westinghouse, with McGuire trucks and Brush bodies. Looking at the lists it really does look as if British Westinghouse had put in a 'loss-leader' type of tender, or possibly not actually losing money, but just breaking even. Certainly the cachet of being chosen for such a high profile order would help promote the company, with the potential additional benefit of repeat orders at a later date. Indeed when the LCC standardised on equipment the chosen electrical equipment was Westinghouse and later Metrovick.

In respect of the electromagnetic and electro-mechanical brake, the British Westinghouse Company really only had one major competitor, the Electro-Mechanical Brake Company (EMB). Both Westinghouse and EMB ensured that their products would fit onto any make of tramcar and be compatible with any make of controller. Thus tramway systems

could up-grade the brakes of older tramcars by fitting electro-mechanical brakes from either manufacturer. The links of the name Westinghouse with brake safety on railways would not have been lost on George Westinghouse. However the type of braking was completely different and so fitted in more neatly with the British Westinghouse Electric and Manufacturing Company than with the Westinghouse Brake Company Limited.

A series of fatal accidents on very hilly routes led to tramway operators looking carefully at brakes. This is discussed in detail in the chapter on brakes; suffice to say here that the Westinghouse Newall brake proved extremely popular and, while figures are impossible to come by, the impression is that the Westinghouse brake was the market leader.

An early customer for the Trafford Park products was the Bath Electric Tramways Limited. (Tramway and Light Railway Society Archive)

Newcastle Tramways also chose Westinghouse equipment. (Tramway and Light Railway Society Archive)

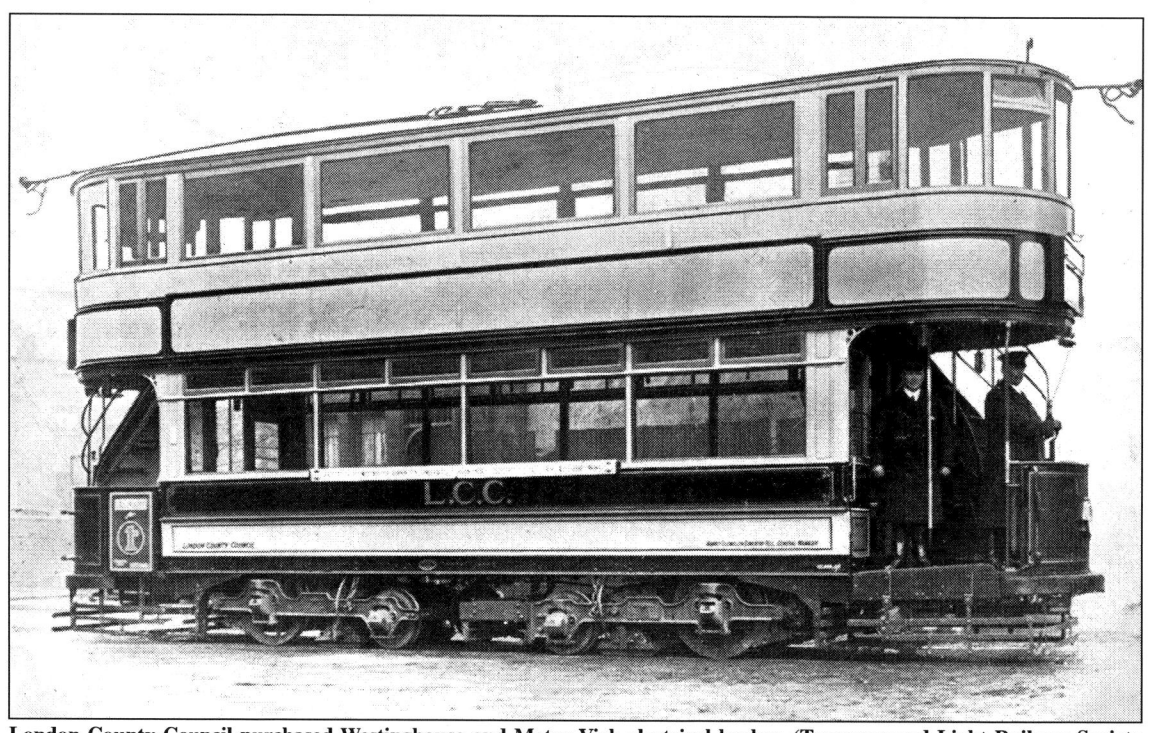

London County Council purchased Westinghouse and Metro-Vick electrical brakes. (Tramway and Light Railway Society Archive)

Chapter 4
TRAMWAY CONTROLLERS AND MOTORS

It was usual on new trams for all the electrical equipment to be supplied by the same company. So the one organisation made the controllers and the motors for the tramcar. In later years, as tramcars were rebuilt and repaired, many had controllers and motors from different manufacturers. There really was no need for both to be made by the same company. So in this chapter I will be looking at the controllers and motors as separate items.

Controllers

A tramcar controller is basically a giant rotary switch with a few extras. It is sturdily built for two reasons, the first is that it has to handle the full electrical power for the tramcar. The overhead voltage was usually around 550 volts DC, and the motors required heavy amperages which need very special forms of switches to control and minimise the arcing that happens when the contacts on the switches are opened. Arcing can be extremely damaging. The second reason is that the controller was expected to stand up to the rigours of driving the tramcar for 12 hours or more a day, seven days a week, 52 weeks a year, with the minimum of down time for maintenance or repair and, in the early days, with no protection from the elements.

The very early controllers only provided power to drive the tramcar, whereas later ones had additional braking positions. Taking the most simple early controller: there are two handles on the controller, both of which can be removed (later controllers had a main handle that was not removable). The handles each rotate a vertical "drum" contained inside the casing. The first handle is small, often called the "key" which fits onto a spigot on the right hand side of the controller top. Then the main control handle fits in the middle of the top. The key can be moved either one position forward or one position back. In either of these positions it is locked on to the controller top and can only be removed by moving it to the central position, with the control handle also in the off position. The central position is the "off" position and no current can flow through the controller. Moving the key to the forward position rotates the small drum and operates switches that allow the tramcar to travel forward, and moving the key to the back position allows the tramcar to move backwards. The latter is rare because when travelling in the opposite direction the driver will usually move to the other end and drive from the front of the tram.

The actual movement of the tramcar is determined by the position of the main handle. Starting from the "off" position and going clockwise there were seven (later eight or more) positions (or notches). The movement of the main handle is determined by a "star wheel" (sometimes called the index or notch wheel). This is a disc mounted at the top of the control drum that has notches cut into it, and a small wheel pushed by a hard spring against the edge of the wheel. The star wheel has two functions. First it ensures that the control handle can only be moved into a correct position with the internal switches either fully on or fully off. Secondly it makes the driver move the handle quickly from one position to another, minimising arcing (and subsequent damage) when the internal switches are opened.

Of the seven positions the

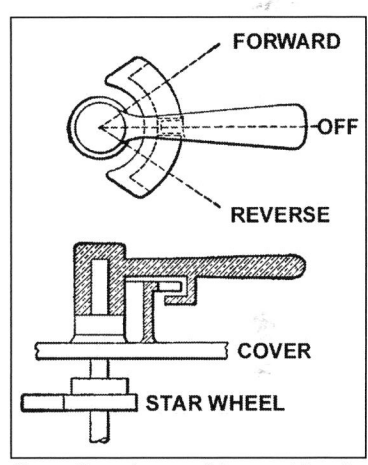

Controller key, without this the controller cannot be operated. (Author's collection)

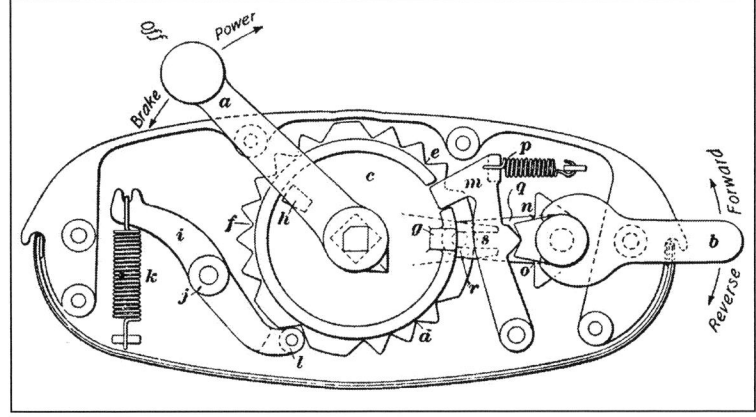

The Star wheel, this ensures that the handle always stops in a correct position. (Author's collection)

The top of the 28A type controller from the preserved Douglas Southern tramcar, showing four series notches and three parallel notches. (Author's collection)

first four are called the "series" notches and the second three (later four) notches are the "parallel" notches. The speed of the motors is determined by the size of the resistance coils the electrical current has to pass through before getting to the motors. In the first four notches the motors are connected across the electrical supply in series, so each motor gets half the line voltage. The first notch has all the resistance coils in the circuit, the second notch has about $\frac{2}{3}$rd the resistance, the third notch $\frac{1}{3}$rd resistance, and the fourth notch has no resistance in the circuit and is also called "full series". In addition to controlling the speed of the motor the resistance notches also prevented the motors trying to take too much amperage. If the motors were connected with no resistances, there would be a dangerously high surge of current that would trip the circuit breakers on the tramcar. This sometimes happened when the driver was too quick notching up the controller.

The distance to be moved from the fourth to the fifth notch is greater than the others, to distinguish it as a different movement. Taking the controller handle from the fourth to the fifth notch does two things. The motors are switched into parallel wiring, so the full line voltage goes through each motor and the full resistance coils are brought into the circuit. Then on the sixth notch the resistance is cut to $\frac{2}{3}$rds, then to $\frac{1}{3}$rd on the seventh notch, and finally the resistances are cut out completely on the eighth notch. This is the top speed and also called "full parallel". Later some operators, notably Liverpool and Glasgow, introduced a weak field diverter. This reduced the field strength of the motors, and increased the speed by up to 20%, but at the cost of lower torque. But it did allow the drivers to operate the weak field diverter when running on full parallel, where speed was required and high torque unnecessary. However, Glasgow discovered that there was a grave disadvantage. Weakening the field strength gave rise to sudden surges in current that damaged the motors. In Liverpool and Blackpool weak field diverters were removed entirely, while Glasgow found an intermediate stage between full parallel and weak field that eliminated the surging.

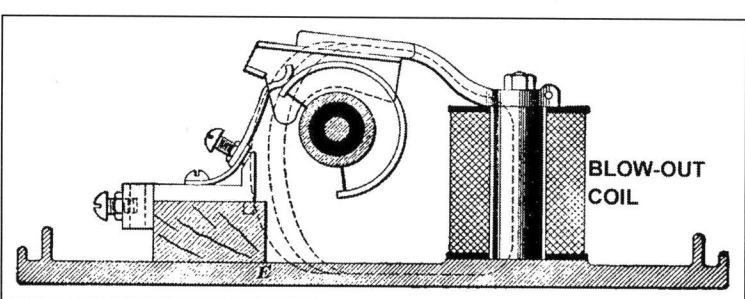

Each contact finger on the controller has a blow-out coil to minimise arcing. (Author's collection)

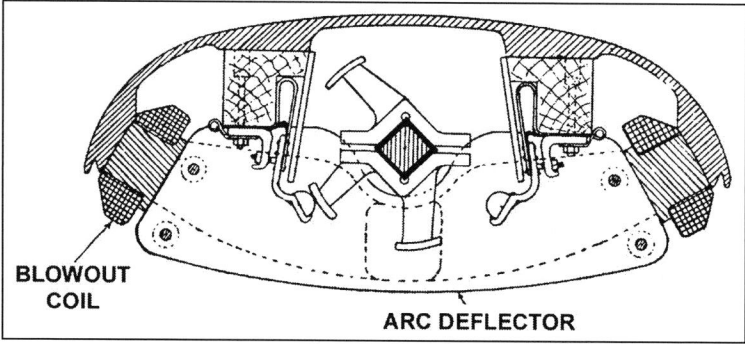

Cross section through a controller showing the contact fingers and relative position of the blow-out coil. (Author's collection)

On reaching the desired speed, or when passing a section insulator, the driver would turn the controller handle back to the off position and allow the momentum of the tramcar to coast along. It is not possible to move the handle back a few notches, like the accelerator on a car, because if the turning motor is wired into a circuit it acts as a dynamo and tries to generate electricity. This either slows the tramcar, or creates current surges which trip the circuit breakers. To resume power the controller had to be turned immediately to the notch appropriate for the speed of the tram.

In the instructions to drivers the tramway operator would always stress that drivers should move the handles as quickly as practical to either full series or full parallel while maintaining a smooth progressive motion. This was to minimise the amount of electricity going to the resistances because the power used only heated up the resistance box. This was of no benefit to the operator, though it did keep the tramcar crew's tea cans nice and warm.

Finally inside the controller there are some special devices and switches. The main device is the magnetic blow-out coil. This produces a magnetic field that helps snuff out the arc caused when the controller handle is moved from one notch to the next. There are also metal plates between the switches called the arc shield to prevent the arc from harming other parts of the controller. Inside the controller case are switches that allow the driver to switch out either motor from the circuits. This is in case of a motor failure. The appropriate motor can be switched out of the circuits and the tramcar can limp back to the depot on just the good motor(s), using just the first four notches.

Fairly soon controller manufacturers started using the motor to slow the tramcar by using its properties as a dynamo. This was done by adding braking notches on the anti-clockwise side of the "off" position. When the tramcar was moving this would adjust the electrical circuits so that the motors were disconnected from the power supply and connected to the resistances. Each notch away from the off position meant more resistance in the circuit. The higher the resistance the more power the motor needed to produce electricity, so the quicker the tramcar slowed. This form of braking is called rheostatic braking. It has several major advantages over the hand brake. First the wheels cannot slide on the rails, because the moment they stop turning the motors stop resisting and the wheels will turn again. Secondly because the operation is part of the controller it has a quicker reaction time from the driver. Finally as the tramcar slows so the braking effect becomes less, so it prevents a jerking stop. The electricity generated usually just heated up the resistances – some operators put the resistances under the lower deck seats to provide heating during the winter (and the summer!). Later some tramcars were fitted with electromagnetic track brakes which were powered by the rheostatic braking, while others used the Raworth system to put the generated power back into the overhead line, thus reducing the amount of electricity consumed by the tramway.

The final change to the controllers came in the interwar period and was the addition of an air brake valve. This was designed to allow operation of all the types of braking (except the handbrake) through the controller handle. A metal box fitted on top of the controller on to which the main handle was fitted. The power operation was exactly as before. The brake application not only applied the rheostatic braking, but also the air brake. Thus emergency braking took no longer to apply than service braking.

During the course of tramway history the motors

The Westinghouse type 90 controller. (Tramway and Light Railway Society Archive)

powering the tramcars became more and more powerful. Correspondingly they consumed more electrical power and so the controller had to be able to handle the increased currents.

British Westinghouse made a number of different controllers, not just for tramways, but also for railways and cranes. The early numbering system appears to have mixed these different types randomly and so the picture is somewhat confusing. The lack of records has meant that the information has had to be built up from details spread among different systems and there are some elements of confusion. One obvious feature of the Westinghouse controller was its height. The controllers were significantly taller than the other makes. This was most noticeable on the London County Council trams where the top of the controller poked above the top of the dash panel. This meant that the control handle had a very straight handle. Other makes had a curved handle to raise the handle knob to the standard height. The reason for the additional height was the design of the controls inside the casing. On other controllers the reversing drum was alongside the main drum. In the Westinghouse controller the reversing drum was concentric and above the main drum.

Westinghouse of America controllers

Until the Trafford Park factory opened in 1902 all Westinghouse controllers were manufactured in America. It is likely that there was a mix of American

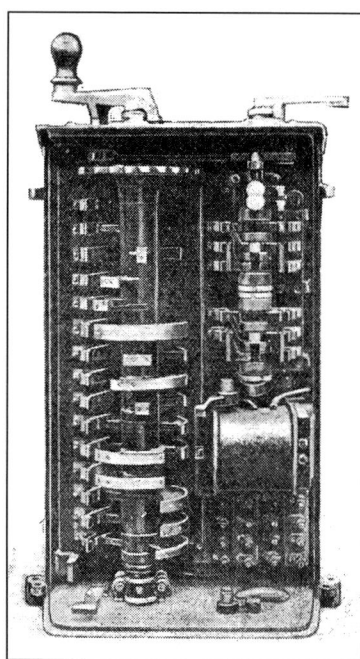

The Westinghouse type 200 controller. (Tramway and Light Railway Society Archive)

manufactured and British manufactured controllers during the period 1902 to 1904 while the factory was being commissioned. I also believe that the outdated 28A controller was probably never made in Britain and any spares or late orders would come from America.

The earliest tramcars had their motors permanently connected in parallel and the only method of speed control was by using resistances. Westinghouse literature implies that in 1891 they developed the series/parallel system of control for tramcars. The controller (number 14) was first offered in 1892. There are no records of any British tramway having any Westinghouse controllers earlier than 1895 when the 28 series was in use.

The 28 and 28A controllers

The no. 28 was the earliest of Westinghouse tramcar controllers used in Britain. The first system to use it was Coventry Tramways on their first tramcars in 1895 and they were then used by the Douglas Southern Tramway in 1896. The controller had only power notches. There were four series notches and three parallel notches. No braking notches were fitted and the driver would rely entirely on the hand brake for stopping the tramcar. It was designed for operating two motors. The no. 28A was introduced around 1897. Basically very similar to the no. 28 it did incorporate a few technical refinements. Sales of both types appear to have stopped by the 1900s.

British Westinghouse and American-made controllers

The introduction of rheostatic braking using brake notches meant a major change in the design of the controller and from around 1899 the new types of controllers were being produced. The extra safety that this gave was quickly appreciated and the braking notches became a regular feature for all controllers from all manufacturers from 1900 onward.

The 90 controllers

These controllers were the 28A controllers with braking notches. Thus there were four series notches, three parallel notches and five braking notches. Again the design of the controllers was for two motors only. The first of this type to appear in Britain were those on tramcars in Hull in 1899.

The 90M controllers

A development from the 90, these controllers gave an extra notch for parallel driving and more importantly two extra notches on the braking. It was claimed that this allowed much more control and sensitivity during braking and the 90M soon outstripped the 90 as the preferred controller from the Westinghouse range. The controllers had four series notches, four parallel notches and seven braking notches. The first of this type in Britain came in 1903 used by the Bath tramways.

The 5915 controllers

Very little is known about these controllers. They are only recorded as being used by Trafford Park Estates Tramways and Imperial Tramways on the Middlesbrough, Stockton & Thornaby system. They were supplied 1901-07. It is thought that the number might be an order number and not a manufacturer's type number.

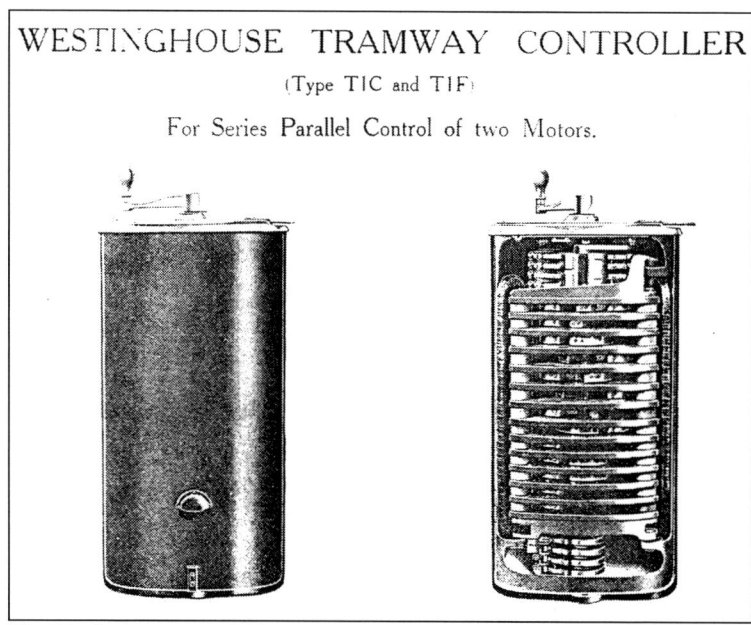

The Westinghouse type T1C controller from a catalogue. (British Westinghouse, Tramway and Light Railway Society Archive)

The 200 series controllers

The 200 series controllers had an additional power notch giving four series notches and five parallel notches with seven braking notches. Presumably this controller was designed to give more control in the acceleration when the motors were in parallel. The additional notch increased the complexity and number of parts used in the controller. Sales in Britain were not as high as the 90M type, so presumably the advantage gained by the extra control was more than off-set by the additional complexity and maintenance. The first recorded use of this type of controller is in 1899 at Glasgow. In Britain the series included types 200, 210 and 220.

The 412 controllers

The 412 type controllers were similar to the 200 series, but built for use on four-motor bogie (double truck) tramcars. The controllers were called "series parallel" controllers – that is the four tramcar motors are connected in pairs in a parallel configuration. Then each pair is connected to the controller as if they were one motor. Hence on the five series notches all motors have half the line voltage, and on the four parallel notches the full line voltage. In addition the controllers had seven braking notches. The need to control four motors required a stronger design to cope with the heavier amperages used by twice as many motors as those used by most other tramcars. The first use of this controller in Britain is 1903.

The T1 series controllers

The T1 series appears to have replaced the 90M and 210 types. T1 were manufactured for controlling tramcars with two motors. Appearing around 1909/10 this series replaced the previous types. They were probably designed to meet the increasing power requirements of the more powerful motors being produced. Otherwise the set-up is the same as the 90M and 210 – that is four series notches, four parallel notches and seven braking notches.

The series carried suffixes, i.e. T1C, T1F, T1R. These represent specially designed controllers to meet particular requirements. For example T1F was made for interpole motors, which need special wiring requirements and T1R for Raworth regenerative controllers.

The T2 series controllers

These were virtually the same design as the T1, the only difference being some slight alterations so that the controller was suited to tramways with an insulated return. In Britain this only occurred on the London County Council conduit system. So British T2 controllers were only seen on London County Council and West Ham tramcars, which made extensive use of the conduit network with through running agreements. Like the T1 Series the T2 carried suffixes for special requirements.

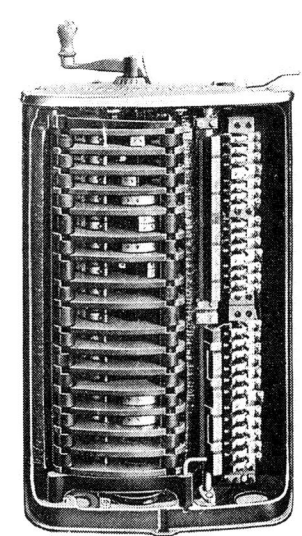

The Westinghouse type T4 controller from a catalogue. (British Westinghouse Tramway and Light Railway Society Archive)

The Westinghouse-Raworth type controller. (Author's collection)

The controller on the restored London County Council no. 106 is not the original fitted to the tramcar, but is a Westinghouse type T2A.

The T4 series controllers

The T4 Series were designed for controlling tramcars with four motors and designated for series parallel control. They had more connections and a heavier rating to take the higher currents required by the extra two motors. They were also advertised as being suitable for tramcars with two motors having a total HP capacity equal to that of the four motors.

British Westinghouse and the Raworth Regenerative controllers

John Raworth was an engineer who had worked with various tramway undertakings for many years. In 1903 he developed a small one man operated tramcar (called a demi-car) for routes with light passenger loads. The tramcar had a number of novel features which required rather special controllers. Between the driver and the passengers was a lifting bar. This was attached to the controller so that if the bar was raised, for example if a passenger went to the assistance of a driver who was ill, he would have to raise the bar. This would switch off the power and apply the brakes. In addition the electrical circuitry was such that the rheostatic braking of the tramcar was used to put power back into the overhead system. This was a moderate success and a company "Raworth's Traction Patents Limited" was set up in 1905. In 1906 Raworth had patented a new series parallel regenerative controller. He had the controller made at the British Westinghouse works. Raworth found that he could modify existing tramcars and their electrical equipment so that they would be regenerative when braking. This was of interest to tramway operators and orders started to come in. Again the controllers for these orders were made by British Westinghouse for John Raworth. Unfortunately for the business John Raworth became entangled in a legal battle with Johnson-Lundell, a company who claimed rights for the regenerative control of tramcars. Although the action was withdrawn it had lasted a year and the legal costs were such that Johnson-Lundell went into receivership and Raworth lost many orders.

For those orders that did arrive the co-operation with British Westinghouse continued for all controller production. Indeed W.C. Moore, one of the Raworth team, moved to the Westinghouse factory, where he worked on multiple unit control, while supervising the manufacture of the relatively small number of controllers made for Raworth. However bad luck dogged the Raworth Company. In 1911 a Raworth regenerative equipped tramcar on the Rawtenstall tramway ran away on a hill and collided with another tramcar, causing injuries to the passengers of both trams. The Board of Trade enquiry blamed the regenerative control and recommended that regenerative control should only be used on level routes. As a result the Raworth Company was voluntarily wound up, leaving 23 demi-cars running on various tramways as their only legacy. The Board of Trade veto put back regenerative control for tramways at least a decade.

Metropolitan-Vickers controllers

When British Westinghouse became part of the new Metropolitan-Vickers organisation

A type T2C controller can be found on Chesterfield no. 7.

the T1, T2 and T4 series controllers continued to be made. A further controller was added to the range.

The OK series controllers

This new series appeared around 1924, a few years before the company became part of the AEI combine. After the links with AEI, British Westinghouse and BTH were part of the same organisation, so there was co-operation between the manufacturers. Although the design rationalisation between controllers from each manufacturer did not reach the similarities that happened with the motors, there was close collaboration. The motors had common numbers, thus both BTH motors type 109 and Metrovick motors type 109 were exactly the same, made to the same drawing and using the same parts. The controllers always had different type numbers thus: Metrovick controllers were all in the OK-B series while BTH were called -B. In the Metrovick controllers there were numbers between the OK and the B. these numbers referred to the order number and so each order had a different number. Hence Leeds had OK9B, OK14B, OK16B, OK18B and OK19B controllers.

Westinghouse controllers in use

The last systems to use Westinghouse controllers ceased operating in the early post war period. From this distance in time it is difficult to determine how they performed in use. London County Council had continued to use Westinghouse controllers and the LCC were renowned for their high standards of maintenance and service. So there could be an assumption that the Westinghouse controllers were reliable and as easy as the other makes to maintain. The only Westinghouse controllers are now in museums and one museum, the National Tramway Museum at Crich, has historic tramcars in regular use. So enquiries were made at the Museum. The controller expert, Brian Pickup, agreed to a meeting and during the discussion he said that he had strong views about the Westinghouse controller. He had found it far more difficult to maintain than those of Dick, Kerr or British Thompson Houston manufacture, the main difficulty being in the replacement of burnt "fingers". These are the contacts that are

The Westinghouse controllers supplied to the LCC had the operator's name and not the manufacturer's.

switched on and off by movement of the control handle. They bear the brunt of the arcing and need regular replacement. Brian told me that it was much more difficult to replace fingers in Westinghouse controllers compared with the other manufacturers. However, he had made a jig which had eased the replacement considerably. These comments must be put in context. There are very few Westinghouse controllers at the National Tramway Museum compared with other manufacturers. Also the use, and therefore wear, on the controllers is substantially less than when the trams were in public service. It is possible that fitters working exclusively on maintaining Westinghouse controllers were able to overcome the difficulties. It is also not possible to determine at the Museum the longer term reliability of the controllers. However, the difficulty of maintaining Westinghouse controllers may have been a factor in the fatal accident on the Bournemouth system on 1 May 1908. The Board of Trade report found that one controller was so

Type 200 controller on the preserved Belfast tramcar no. 249.

The Metro-Vick type OK29B on London Transport HR2 no. 1858.

worn that when the handle was taken off the reversing barrel it was not in its proper 'neutral' position. This nullified the braking of the other controller, allowing the tram to run away down Poole Hill and derail killing seven passengers. Major Pringle's report was severely critical of slack management practices and lack of training to staff.

The last tram controllers to be made at Trafford Park

The very last tramcar controllers to be made at the Trafford Park factory were produced in the mid 1980s. An order came from Calcutta to GEC Traction for 100 CDB2 controllers. These were an English Electric design, a company that had been incorporated into GEC Traction in 1968. No tramcar controllers had been made for many years, so the old designs were resurrected, many requiring redrawing. At the same time the opportunity was taken to contact the National Tramway Museum at Crich. They ordered a small number of controllers which were added to the batch, an exercise that made the production for the tramway museum a practical proposition. When the top plates were cast the designers had left the historic "Dick, Kerr System" in place and added "GEC Traction Ltd". So there are some restored tramcars at the museum with very new controllers. Appendix 2 gives a listing of all the British Westinghouse/Metrovick controllers that can be seen today on preserved tramcars.

Air brake controllers

Although the Westinghouse Empire was built on the railway air brake, and many American tramways used Westinghouse air brakes, British Westinghouse did not initially manufacture air brakes for British tramcars. It is likely that the reluctance of British tramways to use anything more than mechanical or magnetic braking meant that at the time there was no market for them. It was A.W. Maley of the EMB Co. who, in 1922, developed an air brake which combined with the rheostatic brake (previously the air brake was separately operated from a lever set between the controller and the hand brake). Birmingham Tramways carried out trials on two tramcars, one fitted with the EMB brake and one with a Westinghouse air brake. Of course by this time British Westinghouse had ceased, having become part of Metrovick. The Westinghouse brake would have been supplied by the Westinghouse Air Brake Company, which was always separate from the British Westinghouse Company. The EMB brake was

The Metro-Vick type OK37B on London Transport no. 1.

designed to be operated from the control handle, so that on the braking notches both regenerative and air braking would operate. To achieve this an air and rheostatic brake interlock was necessary, which consisted of a metal box fixed on the top of the controller on to which the control handle was fitted. The Westinghouse air brake was operated by a separate lever, just as many of the Blackpool tramcars do today. These interlock boxes could be fitted to any make of controller. So it was possible to see many Metropolitan-Vickers controllers with EMB interlock boxes. Indeed because the interlock box could obscure the controller manufacturer's name, EMB entered into arrangements with Metropolitan Vickers and with English Electric to repeat their names, as appropriate, on the EMB interlock box cover.

Motors

Tramcars and other early electric traction vehicles used DC powered motors because at that time the AC motor produced its best torque at high speed. DC motors had the opposite characteristics, with high torque at low speed – exactly what was needed to accelerate a stationary tram. It is not proposed to examine the different types of motor in detail. The characteristics are very technical and beyond the scope of a general history such as this. However, it is useful to note the general trends regarding motors. The first motors used in trams were open frame. That is, the motor was not enclosed and the rotor could be seen, as could the gear box. This meant that much dirt and grime got into the mechanism, much to its detriment. So a very early development (seen in the no. 12 motor) was to enclose the motor and its gear box in a metal case.

By their very nature motors are part of the tramcar that is well out of the public gaze. Yet they were the reason for the development of electrically powered tramcars. Hidden under the tramcar the only people who saw them were the

Tramway motors, by their very nature, are seldom seen. This photograph shows the tram truck with the motor in position. (Author's collection)

This Halifax tramcar overturned and gives a fine view of the Westinghouse type 200 motors. (Tramway and Light Railway Society Archive)

The Attercliffe factory test shop with rows of completed motors.

Views of the motor by itself. (Author's collection)

maintenance crews in the workshops. In this country the first use of electric motors to power railed vehicles was on the Volk's Electric Railway at Brighton in 1883. Here the motor was constructed around the axle of the tramcar and was very primitive. However, motor technology developed at a fast rate. The American Westinghouse company produced their first tramcar motor (the no. 1 motor) in 1890. At this stage motors produced low torque at low revs so to enable faster revs to be used the motor was double-geared. The gears were enclosed in cases, but the motor windings were open to the elements. A year later they introduced the first commercially successful single reduction motor, no. 3. Then in 1893 they introduced no. 12, a fully enclosed motor giving protection from the elements to the field windings. This was followed quickly by no. 12A which had the refinement of a ventilated armature, keeping the operating temperature lower, and improving commutation. It was the no. 12 that was the first Westinghouse motor to be used in Britain.

The no. 12 motor was a development of the no. 3 motor. It was rated at 25hp and contained many of the features of the former motor, but was much lighter, and the whole motor and gear boxes were totally enclosed. This ensured that the coils forming the rotor and stator of the motor were protected from the elements. As the motors are mounted low on the chassis between the wheel sets they are particularly vulnerable to the wet, mud, and dirt from the road surface. In the early days of the tramcar this had the added element of large quantities of horse dung, a by-product of the other road vehicles which were almost entirely horse drawn.

The no. 12A motor had a technical refinement. The armature winding had a "barrel" type ventilation using longitudinal holes punched through the armature core. This served three purposes. The motor was slightly lighter, from the missing metal. The ventilation kept the temperature of the armature lower, reducing the

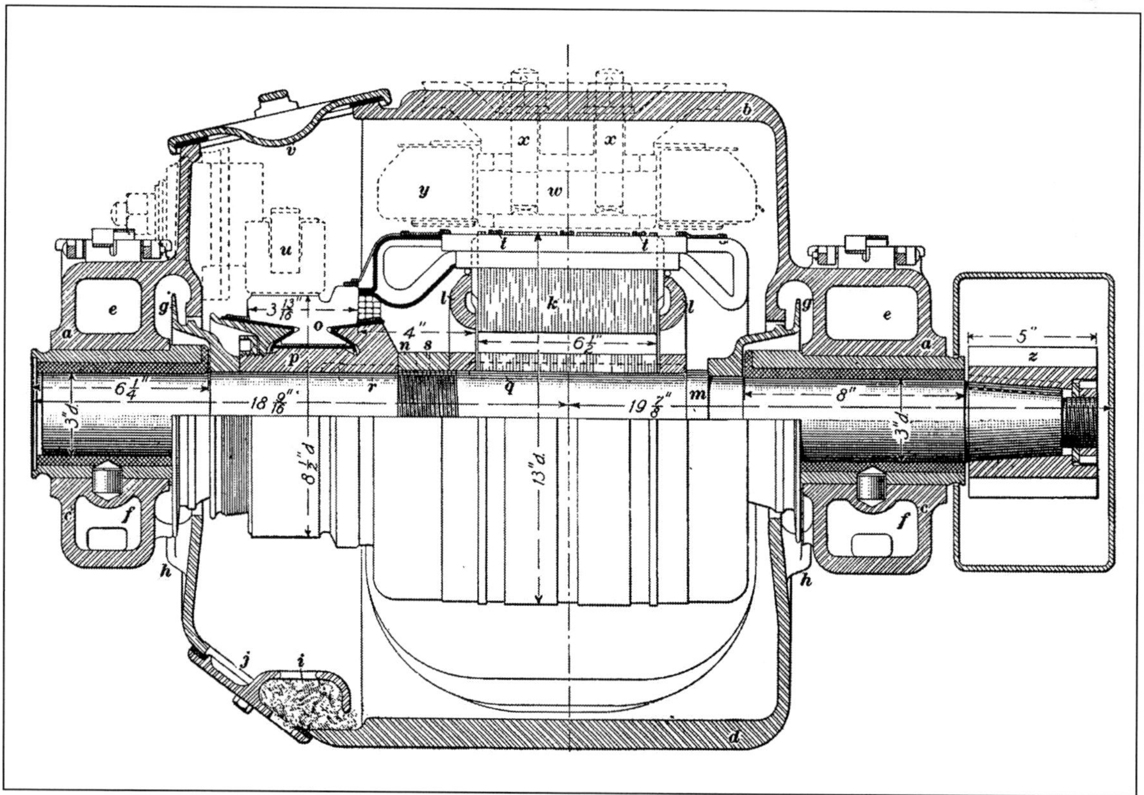

Cross section drawing of the Westinghouse type 200 motor. (Author's collection)

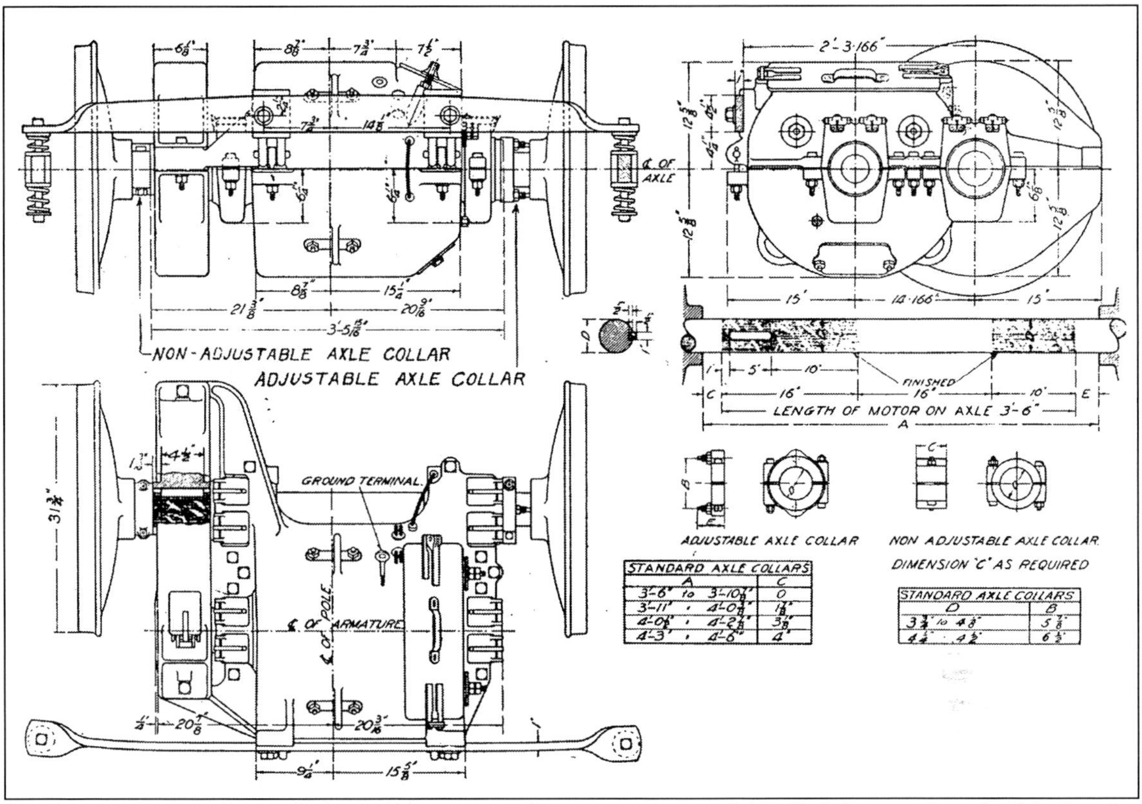

Drawing showing how the Westinghouse 200 type motor is mounted, the gear drive side is hung on the axle while the other side is attached to a sprung bar. This allows the wheels to move up and down on their springing and give sprung support to the other side of the motor. (Author's collection)

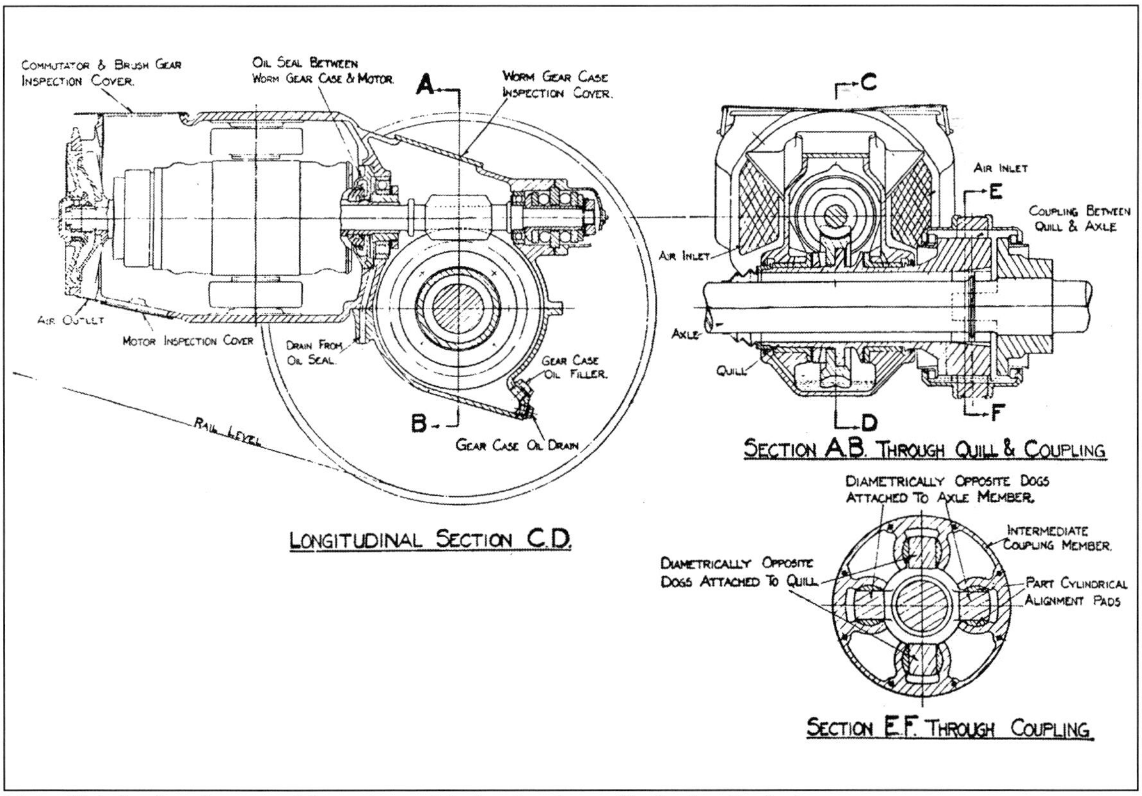

Metro-Vick developed a worm drive motor as this drawing shows. (Author's collection)

The worm drive motor installed in a Sheffield tramcar truck. (Author's collection)

risk of burning out the wiring. Finally the holes enabled the core to be saturated, which improved the commutation and made the motor more efficient. The rating remained at 25hp.

Once the refined design was established further developments could be classified in three families. The first is power. The motor manufacturers were constantly seeking more power and the list of motors in Appendix 3 shows how the power developed from the initial 25 horse power to as much as 60 horse power in later years. Secondly the manufacturers sought to reduce the weight of the motor. The size of the motor was limited by the space available in the tramcar truck. Initially the motor had to be fitted outside the wheel diameter, but fairly quickly the motors were made smaller and fitted between the wheels. Having done that the next search was for lighter motors. This was initially done by using less metal, making holes in as many parts as possible. Initially the metal in the motors was primarily cast iron. Later other metals like pressed steel and aluminium were used, with the manufacturers vying with each other for "lightweight motors". The trend to smaller wheels on tramcars also led to the need for smaller motors, such as the MV 109. Finally the search was always on for efficiency. This was achieved in two ways, by a greater understanding of the electromagnetic forces involved and using them more effectively, and by using the regenerative features of the motor to supply electrical power back to the system. Modern tramways use entirely different types of motors and control systems. With electronic and computer controlled systems the DC power from the overhead is converted to AC to drive the motors, with high power and infinite control speeds.

Following the acquisition of British Westinghouse by Vickers, the new organisation named Metropolitan-Vickers Electrical Company Limited (MV) was restructured, and one consequence was the removal in 1920 of the manufacture of traction motors (including the tramway motor section) to the Vickers Electrical Department in the River Don Works in Sheffield. An armaments factory at Attercliffe Common was purchased, and traction motors were produced both there and at the River Don factory. Design of motors continued at Trafford Park until 1922 when that too transferred to Sheffield. In 1923 it was recognised that the demand for electrical equipment was tailing off and so the production of traction motors at the River Don factory was moved to the Attercliffe Common factory. This was now a self-contained traction motor unit within the Attercliffe factory. By 1928 the demand for traction motors had increased to such a degree that the whole of the Attercliffe factory was dedicated to traction motors with some 800 workers.

There was a further rationalisation in 1928, when Metropolitan-Vickers Electrical Company Limited (MV) and British Thompson Houston (BTH) both came under the Associated Electrical Industries Limited (AEI) Group. It was the policy of AEI that there should be no overlapping in manufacturing whereby two entirely separate factories should be engaged virtually on the same product. So the MV Attercliffe Common factory was to produce all traction motors for both MV and BTH, while the BTH Birmingham works would make all the induction motors.

Production of the Metro-Vick motors was transferred to the MV factory at Attercliffe, Sheffield. This is the machine shop.

Chapter 5
BRAKES

The Westinghouse Empire originated from the success of his railway air braking systems. So it is fitting that one of the best selling items in the tramway range from the Trafford Park factory was the electromagnetic tramcar brake. However, unlike the railway brake, this particular tramway brake was not the brain child of George Westinghouse. The inventor was a Mr F.C. Newell, and the Westinghouse Company recognised the potential and purchased the patent rights from him around 1900. For the first few years Westinghouse advertising brochures acknowledged the source of the brakes with the phrase "Newell Patents".

As with all vehicle braking systems the key to maximum effectiveness is to prevent the wheels from locking and skidding. The friction from a wheel against the surface it is rolling on is reduced to around one third once skidding starts. This is as true today on the cars that we drive, where the introduction of automatic braking systems (ABS) is promoted as a major safety feature. It was George Westinghouse who, by a series of practical experiments, determined the physics of braking. At this time perceived wisdom meant that in emergency the most effective braking was thought to be to lock the wheels and skid to a halt, or in extremes on railway locomotives, to throw it into reverse and increase the skidding. The Westinghouse experiments demonstrated two key principles that have laid the foundations of vehicle braking ever since. First that rolling braking is more effective than skidding braking by a factor of three – that is if a vehicle skids it will travel three times the distance of one where skidding is not allowed to take place. The second principle is that the faster the vehicle is travelling the more braking effort is needed to slow it down. So the braking effort has to be reduced as the vehicle comes to a halt, otherwise it will start to skid. As can be imagined, these principles fundamentally changed attitudes to braking, though as with all new ideas it took some time to become fully accepted, and for many years train drivers were still deliberately locking up their wheels in emergencies.

In the field of tramways, the introduction of electric motors meant that the trams had the power to climb hills that defeated the horse tram. Indeed many of the cable tramways, such as Highgate Hill, Brixton Hill,

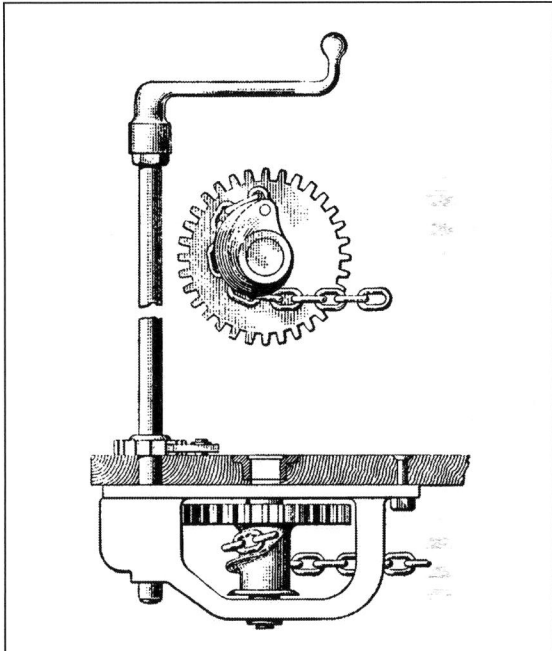

A tramcar handbrake. Note the spindle on which the chain is wound, the shape allows rapid take-up of slack and a strong leverage when the brake engages the wheels. (Author's collection)

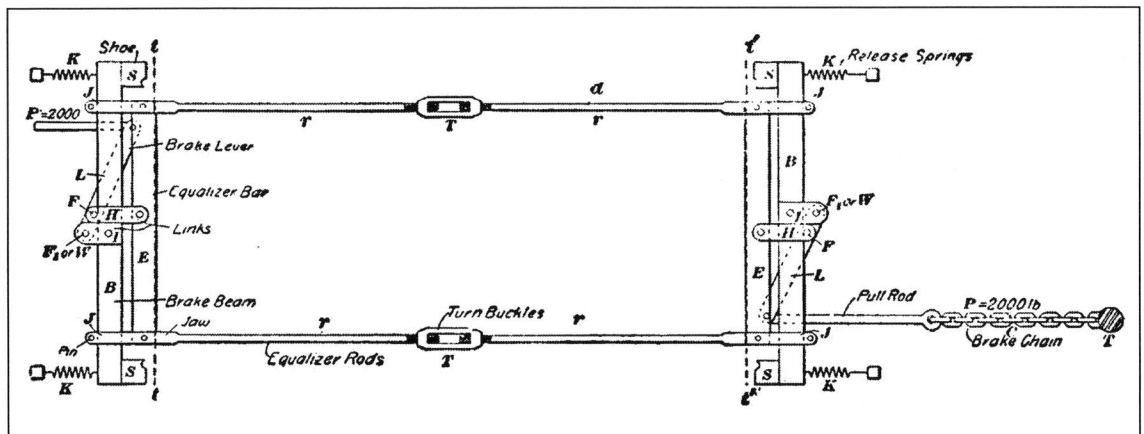

A diagram showing the rodding necessary for the operation of a handbrake on a four-wheel tramcar. (Author's collection)

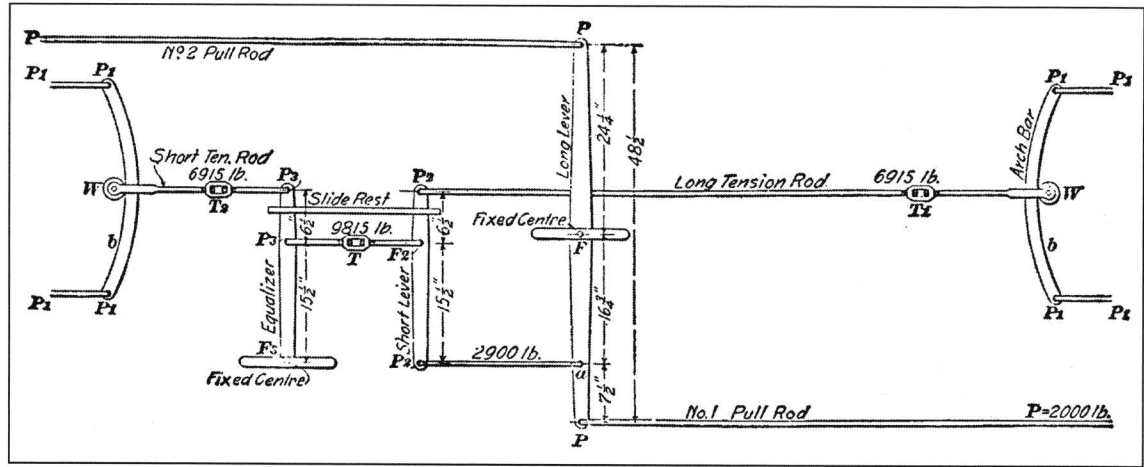

This diagram shows the additional rodding required for the handbrakes on a bogie tramcar. (Author's collection)

Birmingham and Edinburgh were converted to electric operation. However, while the power system was immensely improved, the braking systems did not immediately keep up. The early tramcars relied mainly on the handbrake. After a series of mishaps, other braking systems were introduced and on hilly systems the Board of Trade (the inspectorate) would not allow operation without specific types of braking over and above the hand brake. In addition to the brakes acting on the wheels there were two other types, the rheostatic and the slipper (also called track) brakes.

By the beginning of the 1900s braking was taken very seriously by tramway management, if only because the claims for compensation by passengers injured in accidents caused by bad braking was very costly. In 1901 A.L.C. Fell, Tramway Engineer for Sheffield Corporation, gave a paper on the subject to the Municipal Electrical Association. He carried out tests on the same section of level track using hand,

The overturned Halifax tramcar shows the slipper or track brakes, these are the long pieces of wood seen between the running wheels. By applying a screw they are forced down on the head of the rails. Compare this with the next photograph of a tramcar that is not fitted with such brakes. (Tramway and Light Railway Society Archive)

slipper and electric brakes. The results were:

Speed mph	Distance required to stop the tram in feet	Remarks
12.89	61	Handbrake, rail greasy
11.47	63	Handbrake, rail greasy
10.48	43	Handbrake, rail greasy
14.68	77	Handbrake, rail greasy
9.83	41	Handbrake, rail greasy
14.68	120	Handbrake, rail greasy
11.16	57	Handbrake, rail greasy
14.29	35	Handbrake, rail greasy
14.29	69	Handbrake, rail greasy
12.57	32	Handbrake, rail dry, no sand
11.22	31	Handbrake, rail dry, no sand
14.42	49	Handbrake, rail dry, no sand
8.28	59	Handbrake, rail dry, no sand
14.86	54	Handbrake, rail dry, no sand
11.64	74	Slipper brake, rail dry, no sand
11.64	96	Slipper brake, rail dry, no sand
12.32	102	Slipper brake, rail dry, no sand
14.42	132	Slipper brake, rail dry, no sand
14.42	102	Slipper brake, rail dry, no sand
10.04	125	Slipper brake, rail dry, no sand
12.57	88	Electric brake, rail dry, no sand
12.57	46	Electric brake, rail dry, no sand
12.60	56	Electric brake, rail dry, no sand
12.08	73	Electric brake, rail dry, no sand
13.10	147	Electric brake, rail dry, no sand
14.42	105	Electric brake, rail dry, no sand
13.80	120	Electric brake, rail dry, no sand

Note the electric brake refers to the rheostatic braking on the controller. What is surprising about these tests is the variation in the results. Given that the tests were done on the same piece of track over three different days, the variation is very significant. The difference between the best and the worst at a given speed appears to be double. To my mind these results are inconclusive; however, Mr Fell concluded that the best and most reliable method was to combine the slipper brake with the handbrake, despite the fact that this combination was not actually tested.

In 1903 the Electrical Times printed a series of articles regarding tramway brakes. The importance of the subject was emphasised in the first sentence "The greatest of the unsolved problems of electric traction is, we think, the effective braking of a car."

The different types of braking that were available to operators were:

Hand brakes were a natural development of the only brakes used on horse drawn trams. A hand brake column would be wound by the driver. A chain under the floor of the tram would wind around the column and pull the brake shoes against the treads of the wheels. To help the driver a design was developed where the chain wound around a cone, so that at the beginning the slack would be taken up quickly. Then as more power was required the smaller diameter of the cone gave greater leverage for the operation of the brakes. On electric tramcars the hand brake required drivers to be fit and strong as considerable effort was required to retard a tramcar. However, if too much effort was applied the wheels would lock and skid on the track, with a loss in braking performance. The tramcars carried sand in special boxes, usually under the seats, which, by operating a foot pedal, could be poured on to the rail close to the wheels to increase the friction between the wheel and the rail and hence reduce the risk of skidding and improve the efficiency of the operation. The major problem with the handbrake was emergency use. In a panic drivers were prone to winding the brake on too hard, locking the wheels and making the rheostatic brake ineffective.

Rheostatic braking used the fact that DC motors and dynamos are interchangeable (the electric motor was discovered when an early experimenter of electricity accidentally wired up his dynamo incorrectly and found that it started turning). To take advantage of this principle the tramcar controller was constructed with special notches past the 'off' point. These are braking notches, and when used they changed the connections to the motor turning them into dynamos with the power generated being used to heat up resistors. The energy to turn the dynamos comes from the rotating wheels and has the same effect on them as brakes. So the tramcar slowed down. The big advantage of this type of brake is that, when used alone, the wheels cannot lock and skid. One difficulty is that the braking power reduces dramatically at very low speeds and is virtually nil below walking pace. So it can never hold a tramcar at a stop on a hill. A different brake has to be used for this (in the early days usually the handbrake).

The emergency brake was an extreme form of the rheostatic brake. Here the controller was turned so that the motors were short-circuited and the wheels drove them as generators. This produced an enormous

This overturned Liverpool tramcar is not fitted with slipper brakes, to demonstrate the difference with the previous photograph. (Tramway and Light Railway Society Archive)

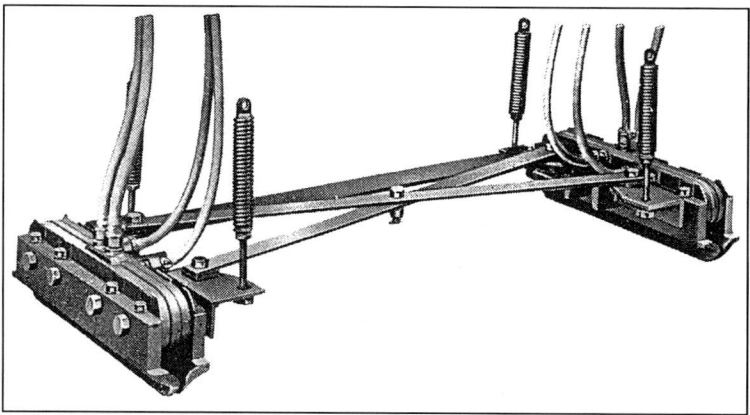

Electromagnetic brakes as made and waiting to be fitted to a tramcar. (Author's collection)

The electromagnetic brake as fitted to a four wheel tramcar. The springs hold the brake above the rail surface, and when the electromagnet is switched on it pulls the block down onto the rail creating a massive braking force. (Author)

braking effect. But the impact on the motors was severe, with a high build up of heat with damage to the commutators and brushes and a danger of stripping the teeth off the drive gears. There were also problems inside the trams as the sudden stop would throw passengers around, often injuring them. However, if it prevented a major crash or overturning then the emergency brake was appropriate.

Air brakes use compressed air to operate the wheel brakes. The great advantage over the handbrake is that the driver operated a small lever and the force of the braking did not rely on his strength. However, it had the same disadvantages as the handbrake, the danger of locking the wheels and skidding.

Electromagnetic brakes fitted to bogies. (The LCC used these brakes as day to day service brakes, while other systems often kept them for emergency use only. (Author's collection)

Slipper or track brakes used an entirely different method. This brake used wooden blocks on each side of the tramcar which were pushed on to the top of the rail. The downward thrust was transmitted by levers from a handwheel, often mounted in combination with the handbrake. Later metal blocks replaced the wooden ones and on some tramcars compressed air was used to press the blocks onto the rails. The effect of the block sliding along the rail gave very effective braking. There was one disadvantage of the slipper brake: in pushing the brake against the rail surface there was a tendency to lift the tramcar off the rails. So the braking effect of the normal wheel brakes was reduced and they were far more susceptible to skidding. It was also thought to contribute to trams derailing (an almost inevitable conclusion of a runaway tramcar, though this may have been a rumour spread by the electromagnetic brake manufacturers).

In 1898 there was a runaway tram in Bradford that left the rails and crashed into a wall. During the accident investigation the Inspecting Officer of Railways, Major Cardew, carried out experiments on the braking of the tramcars. He arranged for a car to roll down the steep hill until it reached 20mph. He then applied the slipper brake alone. He repeated the test for the handbrake and the electric brake. The results were:

Type of brake	Stopping distance
Slipper	179½ yards
Handbrake	64½ yards
Rheostatic	37 yards

Surprisingly the slipper brake came out by far the least effective brake. However in the report Major Cardew strongly supported the use of the slipper brake not for emergencies but for continuous use. He considered that the advantages of having a block of wood pressing on the rail gave greater friction than that between iron and iron. The block of wood was also cheap and easily replaced. He concluded that all the tramcars in the Bradford fleet should be fitted with slipper brakes. Then all tramcars operating on hilly routes (with gradients of greater than

Drawing of the Newell-Westinghouse electromagnetic brake showing that the brake shoes are operated with the application of the magnetic track brake. (Author's collection)

Photograph of the Newell-Westinghouse electromagnetic brake. (Author's collection)

1:15) were required by the Board of Trade to have slipper brakes. However even with this system accidents still occurred. One example of this was the Chatham tramway where electric operation started on 15 May 1902. There were two particularly steep hills on the system, both of which had special operating instructions. On 30 October 1902 tramcar number 19 ran out of control down Westcourt Street and overturned at the bottom of the hill, killing four passengers and injuring another 50. As a direct result of this acci-

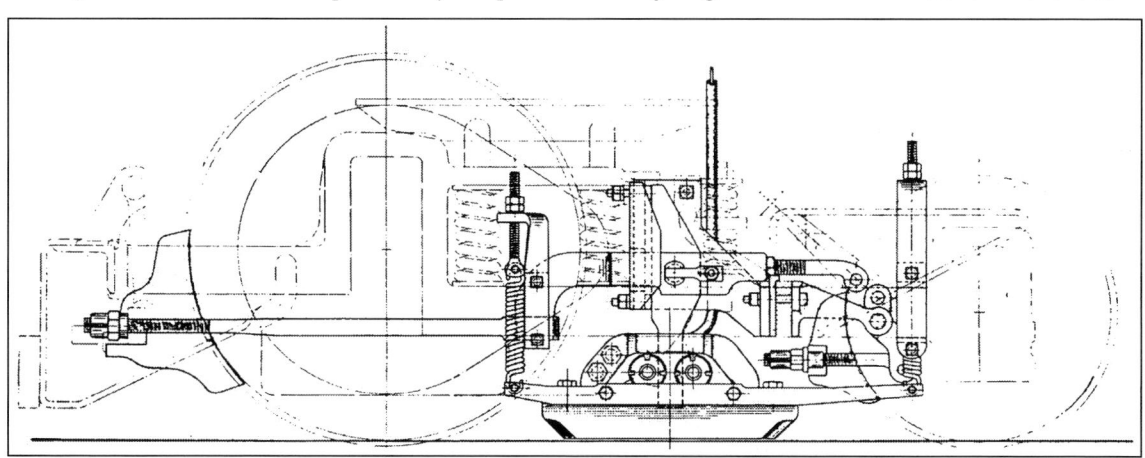

Drawing of the Newell-Westinghouse electromagnetic brake fitted to a maximum traction bogie. (Author's collection)

In 1906 there was a runaway in Archway Road, Highgate on the Metropolitan Electric Tramway. Tramcar no. 115 went out of control and was in collision with the preceding tram. The crash resulted in three deaths. (Tramway and Light Railway Society Archive)

pulling the block onto the rail also exerted a slight pull downwards on the tramcar itself. This helped prevent the wheels from skidding.

The Newell-Westinghouse electromagnetic brake combined three braking systems in one. Operated from the controller in the same way as the rheostatic brake, the first action was to change the connections to make the motors into dynamos. This put the same braking effect on the axles as the rheostatic brake. However, instead of using the generated power to heat up resistors, the power passed to an electromagnet, fitted just above the rail surface, causing it to be pulled down on to the rail. This created the second braking effect by the friction of the electromagnet on the rail surface. A side effect of this was to pull the tram body down a little and so increase the weight on the wheels, thus making them less prone to skidding. In addition the electromagnet was connected by levers to the brake blocks acting on the wheel rims. The levers were so proportioned as to ensure that the wheels did not lock up and skid. If the wheels did lock then the motors would not act as dynamos, the current would cease, releasing the brakes and allowing the wheels to rotate – the danger being that if the handbrake was applied at the same time (easily done by a panicking driver) the wheels may remain locked and the tram skid.

dent the tramway company equipped their whole fleet with Westinghouse electromagnetic track brakes.

The electromagnetic brake was similar to the slipper brake except that instead of a piece of wood being forced down onto the rails, a cast iron shoe was magnetised and this slid on the rail surface bringing the tramcar to a halt. The electricity came from using the motors as generators, acting like the rheostatic brake, except the electricity generated operated the electromagnet. So there were two braking actions – the braking on the axles by the energy needed to turn the motors, and the friction of the electromagnet on the rails. As the iron block was normally held above the rails by a spring, the action of the electromagnet

So it can be seen that the Westinghouse electromagnetic brake was triple-acting: the axles were braked by

1907 was a terrible year for tramway accidents. In April a South Metropolitan Electric Tramways car no.19 ran away down a slope and overturned at the corner of Park Lane and Ruskin Road, Carshalton, killing two and injuring 34. (Tramway and Light Railway Society Archive)

the motors being loaded as generators, there was track braking, and wheel rim braking. These three effects were all directly interconnected and were all electrically controlled. Thus there was no reliance on the strength of the driver. By using the controller to operate the braking there were two advantages. The driver could apply the brakes instantly, and it was impossible to apply the brakes while the motors were receiving current.

The usual-set up had two brake sets on each four wheel car and four sets on bogie cars. They were connected in parallel so that if one had a fault it would not interfere with the operation of the other. Tests carried out on tramway systems showed that a tram going down a hill could be stopped from a speed of 15mph in three-quarters of its own length. The brake would also work as effectively even if the tram lost its power, such as when the trolley pole dewired.

In addition the electromagnetic brake did not rely on working with Westinghouse controllers and motors. It was as effective with all other makes. Thus any tramway system could fit the brake to their existing fleet or include it in the specification of new cars, no matter the manufacturer.

Available from around 1900 it is evident that the first brakes were manufactured in America and shipped to England. The electrification of the Leeds City tramways in 1901 gave the brake a boost.

The first major accident on the Stalybridge, Hyde, Mossley & Dunkinfield Tramway occurred in 1904 when single deck car number 33 ran down the notorious Ditchcroft Hill and crashed into a cottage killing a child. (Tramway and Light Railway Society Archive)

The second major accident on the SHMD was in 1908 when tramcar no. 25 ran away down Ditchcroft Hill and through a wall. (Tramway and Light Railway Society Archive)

Leeds is a very hilly city and the tramways committee were concerned about safety. They wanted to fit the best braking systems to the new tramcars. So they arranged a trial between the three prominent systems then available. They were the Milnes brake, the Spencer slipper brake, and the Westinghouse-Newell brake. The Committee decided that the Westinghouse-Newell brake was the most effective and the first twelve cars, numbers 85, 90, 150-159, were fitted with the brake and used on the routes with the steepest hills. At this date the brakes would have been supplied from America

In 1902 the Chatham accident referred to above, with the re-equipping of all Chatham trams with Westinghouse-Newell brakes, gave another opportunity for Westinghouse to publicise them at an opportune time as the Trafford Park factory was just beginning to be commissioned. A four-page article extolling the virtues of the brake appeared in the prestigious magazine *The Tramway and Railway World*. In the early part of the 1900s the Westinghouse-Newell brake was purchased by many operators, particularly those with routes having steep hills. Notable among them were the London County Council and Glasgow Corporation, two large and very influential customers.

However, the brake was not infallible and in 1906 there was another runaway, this time on the Metropolitan Electric Tramways. A tramcar went out of control in Archway Road, Highgate. On this occasion the wheels of the tram locked, thus no current got to the electromagnetic brake and it did not work. Three people were killed as a result of the accident. The Board of Trade report into the accident suggested "That the whole of the brakes, sanding arrangements,

Another view of the SHMD 1908 accident showing the tramcar resting on the bank of the local stream. (Tramway and Light Railway Society Archive)

&c., on tramcars might with advantage be taken up by the Municipal Tramways Association in conjunction with the Tramways and Light Railways Association." The former was the Association for all council operated tramways while the latter was for company owned tramways. There was no love lost between these two groups. So it was probably not surprising that each decided to undertake their own investigation with the view to have a joint conference to arrive at common conclusions.

The year that the reports were being developed, 1907, was a terrible year for tramway accidents. In April a South Metropolitan Electric Tramways car ran away down a slope and overturned at the corner of Park Lane and Ruskin Road, Carshalton, killing two and injuring 34. In Sunderland in July there were two separate runaways on the same stretch of track, injuring a total of 13 people. In October, a Birmingham tramcar ran away down Warstone Lane and overturned where two died and sixteen were injured. Then later Halifax had a very serious accident in October where a car ran away down Pye Nest Road overturning on the bend at the bottom killing five and injuring 37. Interest again turned to tramcar brakes. This was the major topic of discussion at the 1907 conference of the Municipal Tramways Association held in Leeds. It was Leeds Tramways who encouraged one of their employees, Alfred Walter Maley, to design a new type of electromagnetic brake. In this brake there were also levers on the electromagnet. However these were not connected to wheel brakes, but to a smaller pair of extra slipper brakes, giving more track braking effect. The advantage quoted for this brake was that it could not lock the wheels under any situation and so would guarantee the supply of current. The design proved successful and led to the establishment of the EMB (Electro-Mechanical Brake Company) and for many years a direct rival to British Westinghouse over many of their products. A detailed history of the company can be found in EMB Trams by

1911 was a bad year for the SHMD. In June double deck tramcar no. 44 ran away down Ditchcroft Hill and turned over on the bend at the bottom of the hill with one death. (Tramway and Light Railway Society Archive)

Andrew D. Young published by LRTA in 1985 (itself a reprint of a series of articles in various issues of Modern Tramway in 1984).

Meanwhile the Municipal Tramways Association started their investigation by viewing the previous six years of serious tram accidents. This clearly showed the extent of the problem. There had been seventeen such accidents, of which only one was not caused by brake problems. The two committees published their reports in October 1908. However, the promised joint conference never took place, both organisations suggesting that the Board of Trade should use the two reports to give guidance to tramway operators.

The second accident in 1911 on the SHMD was the worst in its history. Tramcar 24 ran out of control down Stamford Road falling into a railway cutting destroying the tramcar and killing six people. (Tramway and Light Railway Society Archive)

However, the reports gave broad conclusions and neither report gave any recommendations as to the type or make of brake to be used. The Municipal Association focussed on driver error and the need for training and testing drivers plus the dangers of greasy rails, while the Company Association concluded that drivers should be medically fit and that brakes and sanding apparatus should be kept well maintained.

Unfortunately the brake problem had not been satisfactorily resolved and individual operators were left to determine their own conclusions from the reports. The dilemma is illustrated in the views of Anthony Grundy on tramcar braking as expressed in his autobiography *"My Fifty Years in Transport"*. He describes four tramway accidents. The first on 11 October 1904 on the Stalybridge, Hyde, Mossley and Dukinfield Tramway (SHMD), when single deck tram number 33 got out of control when descending Ditchcroft Hill killing a four-year-old boy. The tramcar was fitted with a normal handbrake and a Westinghouse-Newell electromagnetic brake. The Board of Trade enquiry found that the car's equipment was too badly damaged to ascertain the cause of the accident. Four years later, on the same hill, on 2 April 1908, single deck tramcar number 25 (with the same braking equipment as number 33) got out of control, ending up in the river. Luckily there were no casualties and, strangely, it appears that there was no Board of Trade enquiry. Then on 5 June 1911 double deck tramcar number 44 ran away when descending the same hill, killing one passenger and injuring 15. There was a Board of Trade enquiry. In the report the inspector concluded that the driver had failed to carry out the proper procedures and had applied the handbrake, which locked the wheels. Finding that this did not slow the tramcar down he then applied the Westinghouse-Newell brake. Because the wheels were locked the motors were stationary and the brake could not work. Had the driver followed the proper procedure the inspector concluded that the runaway would not have happened. The SHMD

One of the most spectacular accidents was in Scarborough as late as 1925 when tramcar no. 21 ran away backwards down Vernon Road and de-railed and ran off the road through the roof of the Aquarium Ballroom and fell to the floor. Luckily the three passengers and conductor had jumped off the car safely and the driver, who had to be cut out, was not badly injured. (Tramway and Light Railway Society Archive)

The driver of Dewsbury and Ossett tramcar no. 3 lost control of his car going down the Wakefield Road in 1915 running beyond the terminus and into the Scarbro Hotel. The building collapsed onto the tramcar soon after this photograph was taken. (Tramway and Light Railway Society Archive)

Tramway had its worst accident just four months later on 20 October 1911. Single deck tramcar number 24 got out of control descending Stamford Road, derailed at the curve at the bottom of the hill, crashing through a wall and down an embankment and smashing the whole body of the tramcar on the LNWR railway tracks. Thankfully the railway was able to stop all the trains avoiding a further crash. As it was five passengers and the conductor were killed and nine others, including the driver, were seriously injured. The tramcar was equipped with the same braking systems as the previous three. Though little of the tramcar was left after the accident the wheels were examined closely and there was no evidence of any flats, which meant that they were rolling while the tram was running down the hill. What was left of the Westinghouse brakes appeared normal. The controllers were too damaged for any conclusions to be drawn. The inspector made reference to an accident in 1908 at Bournemouth where a defect in a controller led to the brake failure. He then speculated that in the absence of any conclusive evidence a defect in the controller should be regarded as a very possible cause of the accident. Details of these and other accidents can be found in *"British Tramway Accidents"* by Frank E. Wilson published by Adam Gordon.

Four serious accidents in seven years with eight deaths was a major problem for the tramway. Grundy recommended that the Westinghouse brake should be replaced by the Spencer slipper brake. At this time Grundy was Shed Superintendent and the Chief Engineer was sceptical. To demonstrate why he recommended the Spencer brake, Grundy took the Chief Engineer to the heavy works car which was not fitted with a Westinghouse brake, but had a Spencer brake instead. He demonstrated that with little exertion he could lift the tramcar two inches upwards, using the Spencer brake. This surprised the Chief Engineer, who agreed to a test and ordered a complete Spencer brake set. It was fitted to a tramcar which was taken to the Ditchcroft Hill, scene of the first three accidents, for tests. These proved satisfactory and as a further demonstration Grundy took the tramcar on to a level track and accelerated it to maximum speed. Then the brake was applied, leaving the controller on full power. The tramcar came to a standstill with the wheels spinning, as they were unable to get grip owing to the track brake lifting the weight of the whole vehicle off the wheels. Following this demonstration the whole of the fleet were fitted with the Spencer slipper brake and there were no further runaway incidents in the remaining 34 years of operation of the SHMD tramway.

Given the undoubted popularity among other tramway systems for the Westinghouse electromagnetic brake it is worth looking in more detail at both why Grundy felt so strongly against the Westinghouse brake, and why other systems were happy to put their faith in it. I felt that the first question is whether Grundy was correct. Certainly the

In 1905 the driver of this Huddersfield tramcar lost control as it approached the Bradley terminus, and it over-ran the end of the line and came to rest in the front garden of Bradley Villa. Luckily there were no passengers on the tram and the driver and conductor were not seriously injured. (Tramway and Light Railway Society Archive)

In Ramsgate in 1905 the driver of Isle of Thanet Electric Tramways and Lighting Co tramcar no. 41 lost control driving down Madeira Hill failed to take the bend at the bottom and went through a wall at the top of a 32 feet high cliff. The tramcar ended on the beach below. The grooves made by the wheels are very clear in this photograph. (Tramway and Light Railway Society Archive)

absence of any further down hill run-away tramcars seems to support his views. Examining the four crashes shows that in only two of the accidents were any firm conclusions drawn. In 1904 the tramcar was damaged too extensively for any conclusion and the 1908 accident had no Board of Trade enquiry. On the two 1911 crashes the conclusions were that the Westinghouse brake was in perfect order. The failure to operate was due in the first case to the wheels being locked by the handbrake and in the second to a controller failure. In both instances these problems made the brake ineffective. By transferring to the slipper brake the SHMD moved to a system where these particular problems would not have resulted in crashes. The operation of the Spencer brake is unaffected by wheel slip and of course any fault in the controller would not affect it because the brake is operated purely manually. So by changing to the Spencer slipper brake Grundy put in a more reliable braking system.

So what about the other systems using Westinghouse? Well it certainly seems that SHMD were particularly unfortunate in having a series of failures resulting in such tragic crashes. While similar failures occurred on other systems they happened with far less frequency. The major users of the Westinghouse electromagnetic brake were the London tramway systems. But here the use of the brake was somewhat different to SHMD. It was used as a normal service brake while SHMD used it only on descending the steeper hills. So in London all drivers were thoroughly familiar with its use. Also there are few hills in London and those that there are presented a relatively small risk, though prior to the opening of the Dog Kennel Hill route the Board of Trade inspector did insist that there should be no more than one tramcar on each track at any one time. This led to the quadrupling of the tracks to increase the level of service. In fact there was a runback accident when tramcar number 226 was climbing Dog Kennel Hill. The power supply was cut off and the driver failed to control the situation. The tram ran back out of control and collided with tramcar number 1704. Thankfully all injuries were slight.

Birmingham was another extensive user of the Westinghouse brake and there were a number of hills on the system. It suffered runaway accidents in 1907 and 1936. However, both of these were unusual. The first was due to a broken resistance element rendering the magnetic brake unserviceable, while the second was caused by a sudden illness of the driver, who failed to apply the brake.

The most serious accident with a tramcar fitted with the Westinghouse electromagnetic track brake was in Bournemouth on 1 May 1908. Tram number 72, also fitted with British Westinghouse controllers, ran away down Pool Hill, derailing at a right hand curve, crossing the footpath and plunging down a slope into a glen. There were seven fatalities and 26 injured, many seriously. However, the conclusions of the Board of Trade report were that the electromagnetic track brake was not at fault. The reason for the crash was poor management allowing practices that meant the maintenance of the trams was severely compromised. Some two years earlier tram 72 had previously got out of control on Poole Hill and was only stopped by the driver applying an emergency stop using the reversing lever. On inspection it was found that a controller defect had

The Isle of Thanet tramcar lying on the beach. The driver and one of the passengers were very badly injured by the accident. The cause of the crash was probably the driver locking the wheels and going into a skid. (Tramway and Light Railway Society Archive)

been the cause and the controller barrel was replaced by a second-hand one that fitted loosely. On the day of the crash the same controller had locked solid. An inspector had found the controller barrel out of position and he adjusted the pinion gear and freed the barrel, so the tram continued in service. A new driver took over the duties and on his first trip back down Poole Hill, using the controller at the other end of the tram, found no response from the track brakes or the rheostatic braking. Unable to stop the tram using the handbrake the car careered down the hill. Subsequent examination of the controller being used and the track brake showed no faults in that equipment. But the lead to one of the four track brakes had an old break, meaning that only three track brakes were available. When the controller at the other end was examined it was found that although the top indicated that everything was set at 'off' and that the handles had been easily removed when the driver changed ends, the barrel was slightly turned making an electrical contact with the motors. The effect of this was to disable the electromagnetic track brake from operation by the other controller. A full description and the original Board of Trade report can be found in *"British Tramway Accidents"* by Frank E. Wilson.

With their success in sales in 1903 British Westinghouse quietly dropped the "Newell" part of the name and the brake became the Westinghouse Magnetic Brake. Westinghouse had obviously been following the deliberations of the two Committees and the remarks of the Board of Trade. One comment from Colonel York, Chief Inspecting Officer of the Board of Trade, was that a "mechanical attachment" should be developed to allow the driver to apply the magnetic brake manually, should there be a failure of the electrical equipment. British Westinghouse followed this quickly, and within a month had published an article in The Tramway and Railway World describing improvements to their magnetic brake to meet Colonel York's requirements.

Over the years further improvements were made, principally to the effectiveness of the brake. For example the electromagnets were made more powerful, yet needing less current. The unit was made smaller to allow four magnets to be fitted to bogie cars. Better protection was given against the wet, dust and heat. Metropolitan-Vickers continued production of the brake and they produced a comprehensive booklet about the brake in 1924. By now they were able to boast that over 2,000 brakes had been fitted to LCC tramcars, over 1,600 to Glasgow tramcars, over 170 to Bournemouth, 200 to Newcastle upon Tyne, and 170 to Edinburgh. They detailed two types of magnetic track brakes: the "Rocker lever" type and the "Newell" type (harking back to the original patents bought by Westinghouse). The advertisement also mentioned Manchester, Bury, Brighton and Stalybridge as long lasting customers.

These days the brake is found on modern tramcars as well as heritage trams on museum lines. For example the new generation of tramcars in Sheffield have magnetic track brakes as well as automatic sanding and computer controlled automatic braking systems (ABS) which take the brake off if the wheels stop rotating. This not only acts as a safety measure to prevent skidding, but it also minimises the damage of wheel flats. Most, if not all, of recent accidents involving tramcars have been caused by human error.

Chapter 6
FIRST WORLD WAR TRAMCARS

When the country entered the First World War the military hierarchy thought that the battlefront would be a war of movement, that the army was to rely on its cavalry divisions to undertake the fighting, and the battle front would be constantly moving. Therefore in 1913 the Army regulations were changed to officially recognise lorries as the approved method of moving stores to forward units and supplying soldiers in the battle line.

However, by late 1914 the war became a line of trenches where the fighting would continue for over three more years. The cavalry soldiers were no match for the machine gun, and artillery became the main weapon of attempting to subdue the enemy. Hundreds of millions of shells were fired, turning the area into a vast quagmire and paralysing road communications. The favoured lorry became unusable as roads and tracks became impassable. Somehow the vast tons of supplies needed to feed the troops, replenish their armament and keep the trenches in a usable condition had to be transported to the front line. The solution came in the form of a narrow gauge railway system. Initially individual trench tramways were built using wooden sleepers and rails with horse or man power to pull the simple wagons along. Virtually silent, these primitive railways could be used right up to the foremost trenches. It was realised that the best way of moving the materials was by using very light railways or tramways. 60cm gauge (roughly 2ft) was an accepted light industrial standard and preformed rails, rather like a child's train set, could be laid and re-laid quickly according to the needs of any occasion. Locomotives and goods wagons were either available or easily made. So the Government requisitioned what they could and then placed orders with British engineering firms for 60cm gauge locomotives, rolling stock and track. The locomotives were to be of three sorts: the traditional steam engine, petrol tractors,

The reliability of the Simplex petrol locomotive was recognised by the War Department and they were used as a work horse conveying materials to the front line trenches. This led directly to the order to British Westinghouse to be changed from electric tramcars to petrol electric. (Author's collection)

To provide some protection to the locomotive crew some of the Simplex tractors were given armoured bodies. (Author's collection)

The British Westinghouse petrol electric locomotive (or is it tramcar?). (Author's collection)

61

The British Westinghouse petrol electric locomotive in operation. (Author's collection)

The design of the Dick, Kerr locomotive was the same as the Westinghouse with possibly very minor differences. (Author's collection)

Much closer to the front line a locomotive hauls a flat wagon with a heavy artillery gun. (Author's collection)

The types of trains hauled by the locomotives. These also have steam locomotives so the photograph would have been taken well away from the front lines, probably at a main distribution station. (Author's collection)

and electric locomotives. It was envisaged that the steam engines would be used well back from the front line, as during the day the smoke and steam too easily gave away their location, and at night the sparks from the chimney were no better. This would make them too tempting a target for the German artillery.

The War Office decided to purchase electrically-driven trams (in reality electric locomotives) to overcome this difficulty. The idea was to erect a simple overhead, using trolley pole collection, and run supply trains up to the front. At night these would be both impossible to see and very quiet. The steam locomotives would be used further away from the front line, where they were less vulnerable. Some 200 electric locomotives were ordered, 100 from Dick Kerr and 100 from British Westinghouse. The specification was that the locomotives would be 40 to 45HP and be equipped with trolley poles. With the order for the locomotives was another for 200 miles of overhead electric equipment and a mobile generating station. Fairly soon after the orders had been placed senior army officers realised that there would be difficulty in both camouflaging the overhead wiring and in keeping it maintained for use in a battle zone. At the same time Simplex petrol tractors were showing the power and reliability of their motors. So the specification was changed and the motive power became self-contained petrol-electric units. However, they were fitted with trolley pole sockets, as it was still thought that overhead supply might be used. In the event no locomotive was ever fitted with a trolley pole.

Had the original orders not been changed these would have ranked as the most unusual electric tramcars built by British Westinghouse. As it was the locomotives were much more in the tradition of industrial railway types. Although in typical Westinghouse tradition they only manufactured the electrical parts and subcontracted the bodies, frames and even the radiators to the Leeds Forge Company. The first three were assembled by Nasmyth Wilson; however the remaining 97 were assembled by Westinghouse employees, not in Trafford Park, but in an empty factory in another part of Manchester.

Chapter 7
TRAFFORD PARK TRAMWAYS

The gas trams at Lytham St Annes proved to be the answer for the Trafford Park Tramway's first tramway. (Tramway and Light Railway Society Archive)

A better view of a gas tramcar, this one is at Neath. All the tramcars were to similar designs. (Tramway and Light Railway Society Archive)

The story of British Westinghouse at Trafford Park cannot omit the tramway that ran in the industrial estate and provided passenger services for workers in the many factories. The history of this unusual line goes back to 1896. The purchase of Trafford Park by Mr E.T. Hooley in that year has already been described. As part of the plans to develop the land the park required transport. At this time the Blackpool, St Annes and Lytham Tramway was opened by the British Gas Traction Company using gas powered tramcars (they opened their third and last tramway in Neath in 1899). One of the directors of the Estate Company heard about the gas tramway and so the British Gas Traction Company was

invited to build a gas powered tramway across the park from the Old Trafford gateway to the Barton entrance, a distance of some three miles.

The tramway opened in July 1897, after some delays and arguments between the builders and the Trafford Park managers. Four tramcars, similar in design to the Lytham cars, had been ordered and built, but only one was on site and able to be used. During the first week of running the tramcar derailed, injuring two passengers and service was stopped. The service did not resume until April of the following year, which coincided with a six-week run of the Barnum and Bailey's Circus in the Park grounds.

The following year, 1899, saw no better fortunes for the tramway. In November the British Gas Traction Company went into liquidation owing monies to Salford Corporation gas works. So the gas supply was cut off, and without fuel the tramcars stopped running for the second time. The Trafford Park Estates Company acted swiftly, purchased the tramway, restored the gas supply and got the tramway running again within the week. Now that the Estates

One of the original Neath gas trams has been preserved and is restored as a static display in South Wales. (Author's collection.)

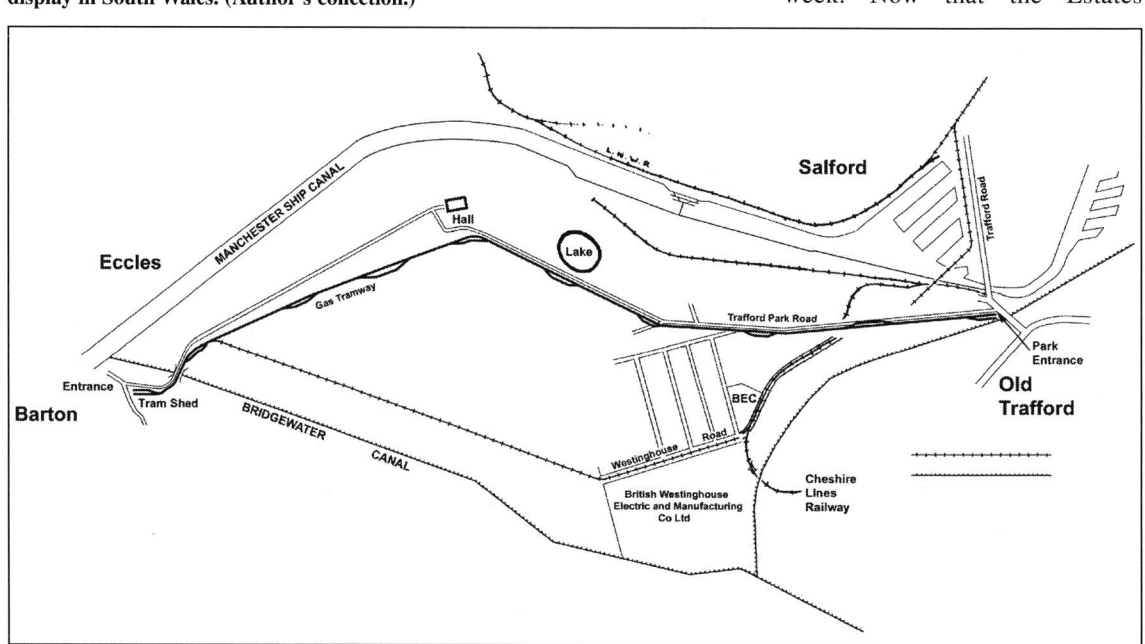

Map of the gas tramway. The Trafford Park owners hoped that many more industrial units would be built across the park and the Barton entrance would be well used. In practice the factories grouped near access to the railways and canals and hence stayed on the Old Trafford side. (Tramway and Light Railway Society Archive)

Company had control of the trams they expanded the scope of the transport by purchasing horse buses to add to the tram services. However they discovered a major difficulty with the tramway. It had been built on the basis that the industrial concerns building their factories in the Park would spread out over the park and would seek access to the canal. In reality the companies that moved in crowded towards the Trafford Park Gates entrance in Salford. This was because the access to the labour market in Trafford and Manchester was better, and rather than seek access to the canal, they sought to have access to the Cheshire Lines

One of the Trafford Park gas tramcars. (Tramway and Light Railway Society Archive)

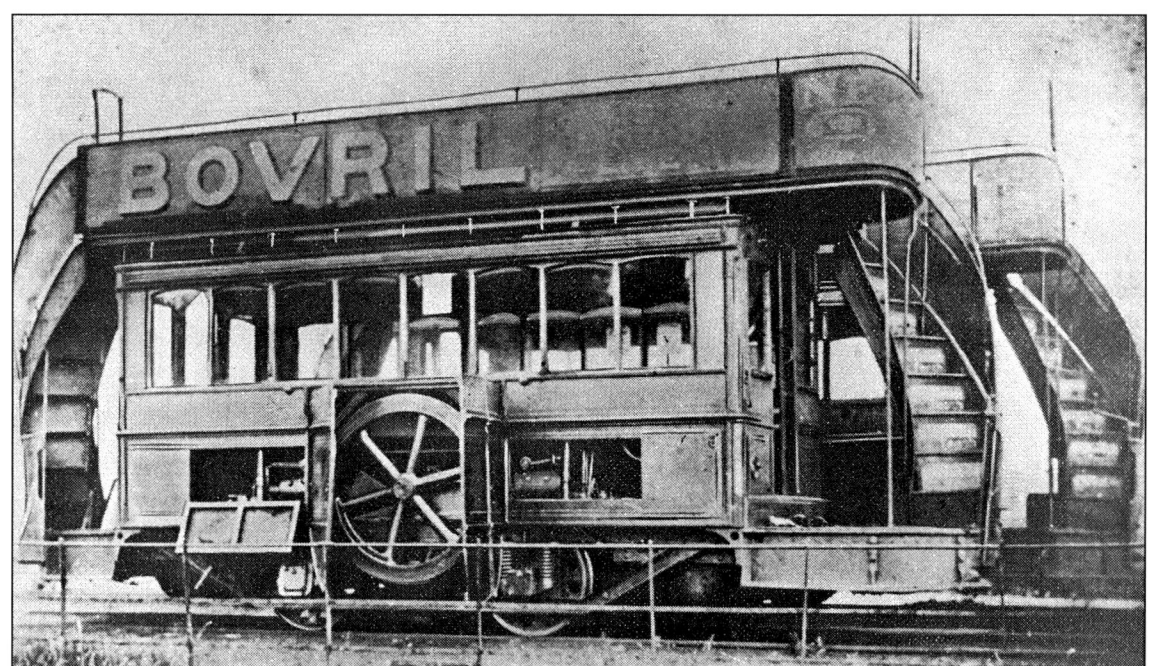

Two of the Trafford Park trams side by side with one having the maintenance panels open, showing the mechanism and flywheel. (Tramway and Light Railway Society Archive)

Railway. The sites they chose were not on the gas tram route. So the tramway did not get the anticipated numbers of passengers.

One of these companies was British Westinghouse. Not surprisingly the Estate Company realised that British Westinghouse was expanding its supplies of tramway materials to British tram systems, so they approached the factory with the idea that British Westinghouse could take over the tramway and electrify it. But the factory was not interested, so the Estate Company

The gas tramway in action. (Tramway and Light Railway Society Archive)

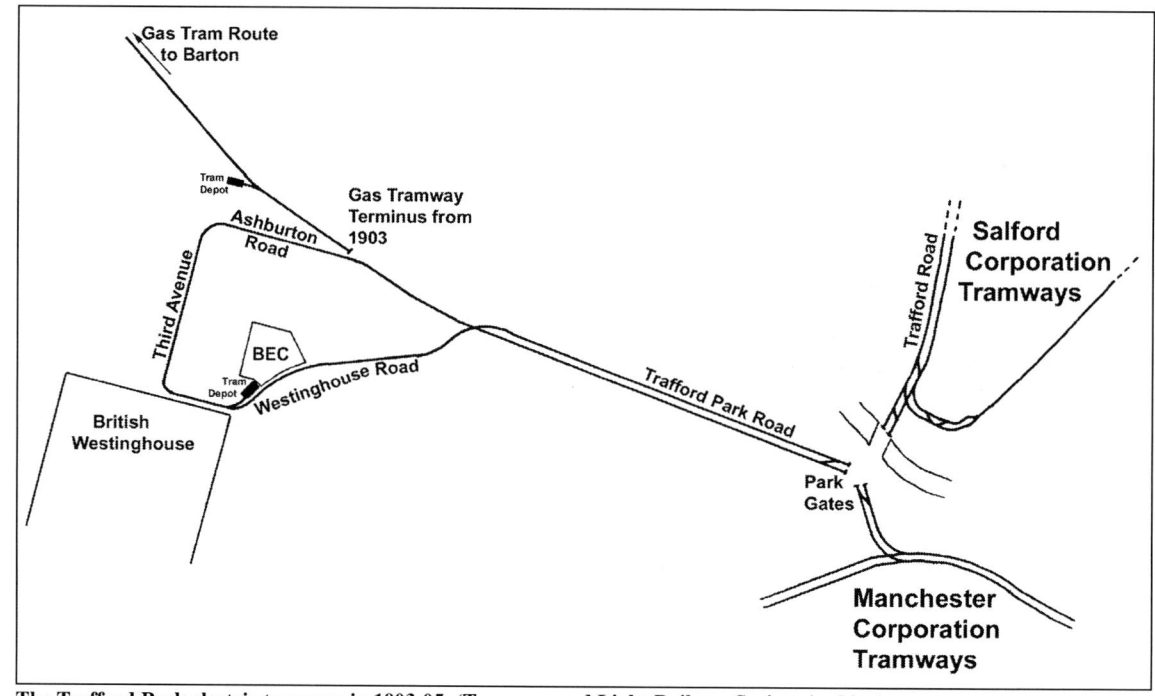

The Trafford Park electric tramway in 1903-05. (Tramway and Light Railway Society Archive)

A Trafford Park tramcar waits by the post office. This is close to the terminus of the old gas tramway. (Tramway and Light Railway Society Archive)

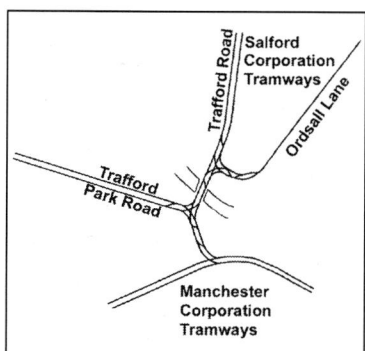

In 1905 the tramway was linked to the Manchester and Salford systems. (Tramway and Light Railway Society Archive)

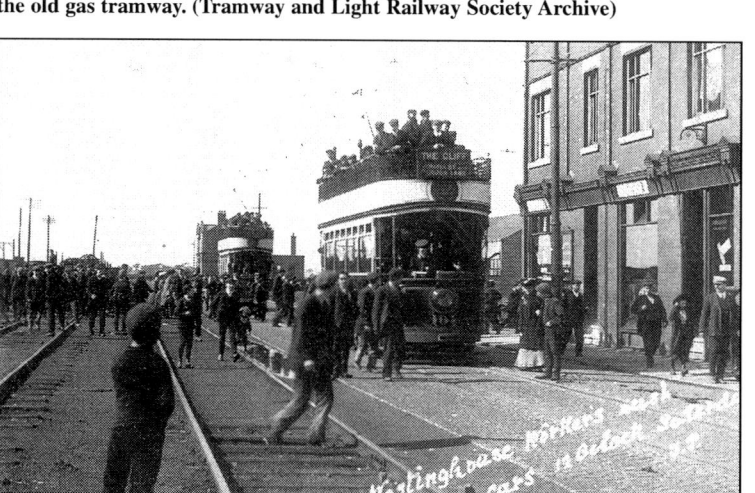

Salford tramcars ready to pick up workers in Westinghouse Road. (Tramway and Light Railway Society Archive)

made approaches to Manchester and Salford Corporations and South Lancashire Tramways Company, but nothing came of any of these offers.

In 1901/02 the British Electric Car Company built and opened a new factory close to the Westinghouse works in Trafford Park. In 1902 the Estates Company decided to build an electric tramway to serve the ever-expanding factories on the eastern side of the park. The route went from the entrance in Trafford Road along Trafford Park Road, forked left into Ashburton Road, then turned left on to Third Avenue, another left turn into Westinghouse Road, and up to Trafford Park Road and back to the entrance, a total of about 2½ miles. Five blue and white, four-wheel tramcars (numbers 5-9) were ordered from the British Electric Car Company, with British Westinghouse electrical motors, controllers and other equipment. The new lines opened in 1903, with the gas trams still operating from a new foreshortened terminus near Ashburton Road to the old terminus at Barton. The service was extremely successful and the numbers of workers carried was such that a fifth tramcar was ordered. This was an open-top bogie car, again built by the British Electric Car Company, to the same design as new trams being built for Salford Corporation. This tram was painted in the Salford livery of maroon and white and not the blue and white of the first five trams. A further vehicle was purchased, this being a very long single deck trailer. Again it was built by British Electric Car Company. Though its extra carrying capacity was very useful – it carried up to 100 workmen – it also proved cumbersome to operate. To make it more useful it was decided in 1904 to add a top deck to the trailer and to motorise it. When completed this became the largest tram in Britain, with a seating capacity of 132. In practice the tramcar would be filled with every worker waiting at the stop, the principle being never to leave anyone behind. The crowded conditions soon led to it gaining the nickname the cattle truck.

The British Electric Car Company was fated to have a short life. It ran into financial difficulties and was put into liquidation late in 1903, finally closing completely in 1904. The premises remained empty until taken over by the Ford Motor Company in 1911.

The Trafford Park Estate Company continued to try and persuade Salford and Manchester Corporations to take over the park tramway. In 1904 they gained agreement for the line to be connected at the entrance to the newly laid tram tracks joining the

The Park had a royal visit in 1905 and the entrance was heavily decorated for the event. The Trafford Park trams wait under the gates, at this time the track connection to the Manchester and Salford systems had been made, but there was no through running agreement until the October. (Tramway and Light Railway Society Archive)

The mix of railed transport in the park is very evident in this photograph with the tramway alongside two tracks of goods railway. The double headed goods train is composed of underground carriages bound for the Bakerloo line. (Tramway and Light Railway Society Archive)

Just before clocking off time at the Westinghouse factory, Salford trams would line up ready to take the rush of workers going home. (Tramway and Light Railway Society Archive)

two Corporation systems. They reached agreement with Salford and Manchester to have the connection built, and for the two Corporations to operate their trams in the Park. However the connection was delayed and to hasten the event the Estates Company threatened to sue the two Corporations for breach of contract, and they also began preparing a Parliamentary Bill to have powers to run their trams into Manchester. These actions focussed the minds of the Corporations and within a month (by February 1905) the rail connection was made. However the Corporation cars did not start running through services into the Park until October 1905.

Then in 1905 Salford Corporation agreed to buy all the Estate Company electric tramcars. From this point the Estate Tramway became part of the Salford Corporation system and was served by trams from that Corporation and by Manchester. They incorporated the line into their routes, and workers no longer had to change trams at the Park entrance, but could ride all the way to their factory. This left the gas tramway, which was still operated by the Estate Management, but it was now getting very old and worn out. It struggled on for another couple of years, finally closing in 1908. The service was taken over by a locomotive and two carriages forming a workman's train that operated twice in the morning and once in the evening. This ran until 1921 when it was discovered that the train was operating illegally. So it was removed and replaced by a bus service.

The electric tramway continued to be operated by Salford and Manchester for many years, although there was a decline as some of the tram routes were replaced by bus services. The last tram ran in Trafford Park in 1946, with all the subsequent public transport being provided by buses.

Salford and Manchester tramcars in Third Avenue with the British Westinghouse water tower in the background. (Tramway and Light Railway Society Archive)

A long line of Manchester and Salford trams wait for the evening rush in Westinghouse Road. (Tramway and Light Railway Society Archive)

A modern Manchester tramcar in Trafford Park in 1939. (Tramway and Light Railway Society Archive)

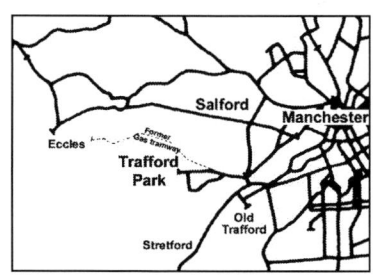
The tramway plan in 1929 showing the relationship between the park tramway and the Manchester and Salford systems. (Tramway and Light Railway Society Archive)

Chapter 8

METROPOLITAN-VICKERS ELECTRICAL COMPANY LIMITED AND ASSOCIATED ELECTRICAL INDUSTRIES

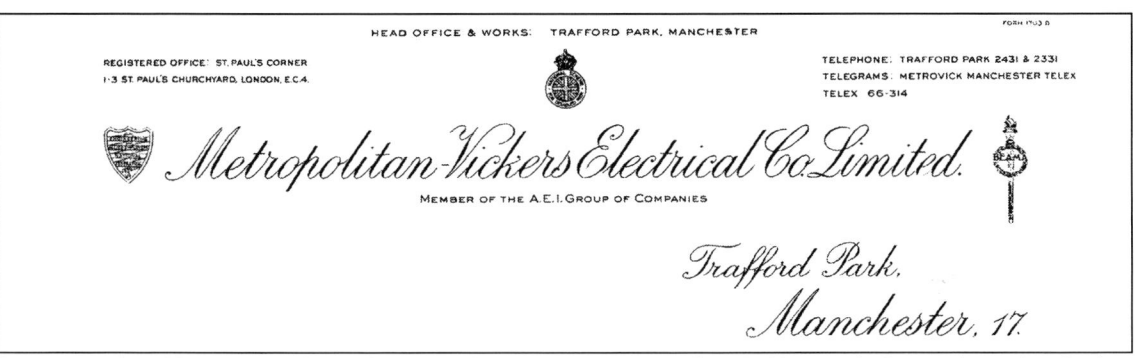

Letterhead of the Metropolitan Vickers Company after the change of name from British Westinghouse. (Author's collection)

The world of George Westinghouse had a catastrophic year in 1907. Having built a massive empire with factories in many countries, the financial structure showed its disastrous weaknesses in this year. Three of his major companies went into receivership. These were The Westinghouse Electric Company, The Westinghouse Machine Company, and the Westinghouse Security Investment Company. Of these the Electric Company was the largest by far. It collapsed owing $43 million with total liabilities of $70 million. This was in 1907 – the equivalent today would be far greater. At the time it was considered to be the greatest failure in American history. Surprisingly the company continued trading, and George Westinghouse himself formulated the recovery plan, although it took fourteen months to establish it. Basically the creditors took shares in the company in settlement of their claims. This was done by increasing the numbers of shares, and what it did was to reduce the debt by a third, eliminating the interest charges to an amount the company could meet. In addition a subscription of $6 million was called for. George Westinghouse provided $1.5 million of this and 5,000 of his employees subscribed a further $600,000. The impact of this on George Westinghouse is explored further in chapter 9.

Despite the problems in America, 1907 was a good

The Metropolitan Vickers Company logo. (Author's collection)

The full Metropolitan Vickers Company trade mark. (Author's collection)

On publicity material they often incorporated a silhouette of the Trafford Park factory with the logo. (Author's collection)

69

year for British Westinghouse. Following earlier financial problems George Westinghouse had introduced Philip Lange from America to review the situation in 1906. In the event Lange stayed to become General Manager. By cutting back on excessive management he was able to turn the company around. But late in 1907 came the news of the American company's receivership. The American company owned a considerable proportion of British Westinghouse and backed the financing of the British company. The banks became concerned and sought additional security for their loans. It was very much in the balance whether the British firm would be pulled down. But visits to the major bankers reassured them, and a mortgage of £250,000 was raised to keep the factory going. The American company still continued to own more than 50% of the British company. However, their influence declined as a result of their financial problems, and this was compounded when George Westinghouse died in 1914. The British company was seeking greater association with Britain and in 1916 sought admission to the newly formed Federation of British Industries.

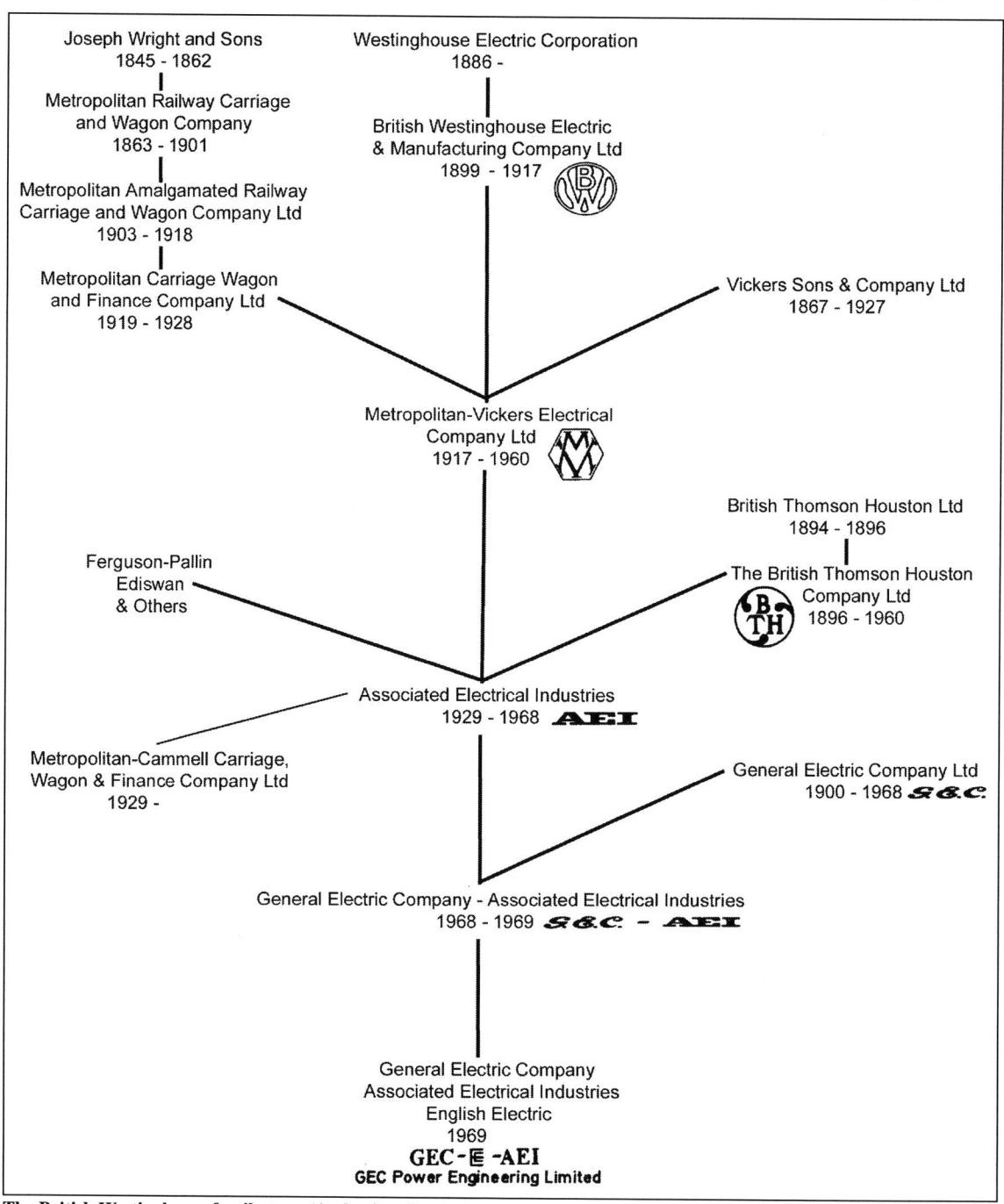

The British Westinghouse family tree. (Author's collection)

ELECTRICAL EQUIPMENT
of the
MODERN TRAMCAR

Rotterdam Electric Tramways Tramcar with trailercar in service.

METROPOLITAN-VICKERS ELECTRICAL CO. LTD.
TRAFFORD PARK, MANCHESTER, ENGLAND

1,000.4.52   *FORM 5713*   7850/3

Front page of a booklet with modern tramway products. (Author's collection)

Glasgow Cunarder tramcar, the 100 tramcars of this class were all built with Metro-Vick motors and control equipment. (Author's collection)

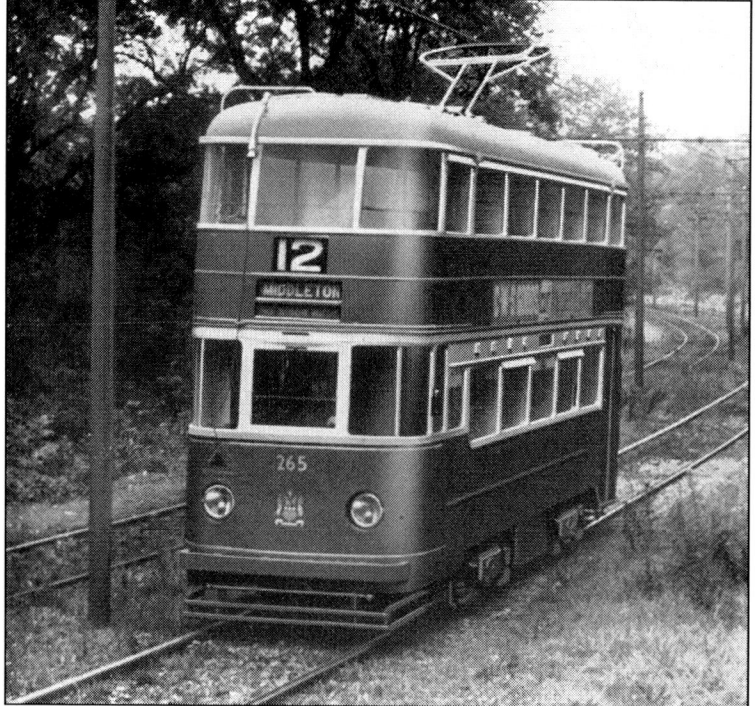

Leeds Middleton Bogies had Metrovick control gear and motors. (Author's collection)

This was declined because the company was still under American control. The British company then decided to sever the control from America and become entirely British. To this end they sought the help of Frank Dudley Docker, who was a founder of the Federation of British Industries. A British holding company was formed (Electric Holdings) and in 1918 this bought out the American shares for £1,200,000, the capital being found by The Metropolitan Carriage, Wagon and Finance Co., owned by Docker. However, Docker had aspirations to be the nucleus of a British electrical giant, and started by exploring the possibility of buying the British end of the Siemens business from the Custodian of Enemy Properties and they also explored merging with GEC. However, these proposals fell through. So then thoughts turned to collaboration with Vickers Limited. In 1919 Frank

Docker sold his Metropolitan Carriage Wagon and Finance Co., with its controlling interest in British Westinghouse, to Vickers Electrical Co. Limited for £13 million. The new combine was called Metropolitan-Vickers Electrical Co. Ltd, officially shortened to Metrovick. The new company continued to supply electrical equipment for rail transport as well as many other uses. Another strong product of the combine was the electric lamp through the Edison Swann Company.

To begin with the post war period was difficult for the company, with restrictions of imports and materials. The depression years continued to be difficult until in 1926 the Central Electricity Board was formed. The National Grid was started, and this resulted in many orders for heavy equipment to service the grid. At the same time exports developed and the company was in a period of considerable profit. The tramway items continued to be produced, though at a lesser rate than before. The time from the end of the First World War saw a decline in British street tramways. Many of the systems had suffered during the war from lack of materials, men and maintenance. The omnibus and petrol lobbies were gaining power, and corporations were being persuaded to cut back or even close their tramways in favour of bus services. So the demands for tramway products lessened dramatically. However, the rolling stock that was in use was growing old and much of the electrical equipment needed replacing, particularly as the new motors and controllers were lighter, more powerful and less costly to run. So manufacture of motors and controllers continued, even though they were being put into old tram bodies.

Then in 1928 the Vickers Group decided to sell Metrovick to the International General Electric Company of America. This was part of a much larger plan to create a massive amalgamation of three or four big electrical manufacturing concerns. In the event the only one to join Metrovick was British Thompson-Houston (BTH). The International General Electric Company set up Associated Electrical Industries (AEI) as the holding company to bring together Metrovick, BTH, Ferguson, Pailin Ltd and the Edison-Swann Electrical Company Ltd, although each company continued to trade under its own name, with AEI being a financial holding company. However there was, to use modern terminology, rationalisation. Production of all electric motors was moved to the Metrovick Attercliffe factory in Sheffield. Designs were unified, and as motors came off the production line they were given either Metrovick or BTH labels depending under which company name the initial order had been made. However, there was a high degree of competitive rivalry between Metrovick and BTH. Despite efforts by AEI the rivalry continued for many years.

Metrovick was under considerable pressure during the Second World War, contributing heavily to

A Metro-Vick low voltage master controller fitted to the Glasgow Cunarder Class. (Author's collection)

Sheffield Roberts type tramcar fitted with Metrovick motors and resilient gears. (Author's collection)

Interior of the Sheffield tram, using Metrovick fluorescent lighting. (Author's collection)

Front page from a booklet on magnetic brake equipment featuring London County Council tramcars. (Author's collection)

the war effort including building 1,000 Lancaster heavy bombers. After the war the commercial rivalry with BTH continued. In 1945 Oliver Littleton (later Lord Chandos) became Chairman of AEI and made a significant improvement in the efficiency and productivity of the group. But he failed to reduce the competitive rivalry between the two organisations. An example of this came in 1946 when Glasgow sought quotes for 100 motors for its new Mark II Coronation (Cunarder) tramcars. The lowest tenders came from both Metrovick and BTH, both equally priced. So the Corporation decided to split the order giving half to each company. The first problem came when the Corporation discovered that by lowering the numbers to each company the price went up. Then Metrovick made representations on the basis that they had lost out on previous bulk orders despite doing initial research. So Glasgow Corporation decided to give the order for all 100 motors to Metrovick. A strange situation, when the motors were all made in the same factory on the same production line, but indicative of the relationship between the companies.

Metrovick's post-war position was one of increased expansion with the construction of new factories and the internal alteration of existing ones. As the diversity and extent of AEI's products expanded, the Company was joined by Sunvic Controls (1949), Birlec (1954), Siemens Brothers (1955), W.T. Henley (1958) and London Electric Wire Company & Smiths (1958). The vast market for generating equipment after the war was extremely lucrative for Metrovick, but its competitiveness with BTH intensified. The project at Larne in Northern Ireland, completed in 1957 by BTH, involved the construction of the largest turbine works in Europe. It was hoped by BTH that the production of turbo-generating sets in the works at Larne would surpass that of the existing factory at Rugby. This enterprise was resented by

Metrovick who constructed a transformer factory at Wythenshawe, costing £2.5 million, at a fraction of Larne's £8 million price tag. Despite BTH's new plant at Larne, Metrovick was progressing competitively in the turbine business. Relations between the two rivals again deteriorated when BTH secured the contract for the Buenos Aires power station worth £35 million. Throughout the 1950s Metrovick became established in the manufacture of domestic appliances such as refrigerators and cookers, which became a profitable enterprise for the company. As already mentioned, during his second period as Chairman of AEI (1954-1963) Lord Chandos resolved to extinguish the internal competition between BTH and Metrovick. The regeneration of AEI was the major goal for Lord Chandos but he failed to achieve it and his successive attempts at reorganising AEI were ineffectual. In 1959 AEI became a trading company and the AEI symbol began to replace most of the brand names and trademarks of companies within the group. It was Lord Chandos' struggle to suppress the disorder and conflicting rivalry within AEI that led to the long-established names of British Thomson-Houston and Metropolitan-Vickers being eliminated from the electrical industry on 1 January, 1960. This was resented by many Metrovick and BTH employees. The remaining years of Chandos' reign were difficult ones for both himself and AEI. In removing the old names, AEI experienced a decrease in profits and share values on the stock market. The indecisiveness of the board and executives at AEI did not assist the company through this turbulent period, as little action was taken to resolve AEI's structural problems. Though Lord Chandos' policies were essential to reassert AEI's dominance in the electrical industry, the elimination of the customary names of British Thomson-Houston and Metropolitan-Vickers was deemed unnecessary by those in the engi-

Edinburgh tramcar that used Metrovick magnetic brakes. (Author's collection)

Glasgow was another extensive user of the Metrovick magnetic brakes. (Author's collection)

neering world. Lord Chandos had particular problems from 1960 to 1963, leading to his resignation in 1963 at the age of seventy. The following two years saw profits but then the company had a disastrous year in 1966. In 1967, the General Electric Company's Arnold Weinstock and the Chairman of the Industrial Reorganisation Corporation, Ronnie Grierson, proposed an instant solution to the company's problems. This was to culminate in the historic £120 million bid by GEC for AEI, resulting in a merger in November 1967. The following year the new organisation merged with English Electric, incorporating Elliott Bros., The Marconi Company, Ruston and Hornsby, Stephenson, Hawthorn & Vulcan Foundry, Willans and Robinson and Dick, Kerr.

The amalgamations of companies led to an unusual use of names. In 1979 the Westinghouse Brake & Signal Company supplied the solid state thyristor control for Blackpool number 761, a new tram created from an accident-damaged Balloon car. By the time the next tram, 762, was built in 1982 the company had been absorbed into the Hawker Siddeley Group. So car 762 and the whole of the following 'Centenary' class (641-648) were equipped with identical equipment, but it carried the name 'Brush'.

In 1985 GEC Traction had an extra 'Centenary' class car built, number 651, to test out a switched reluctance motor control system that was developed by ex Metropolitan Vickers staff.

By now the old British Westinghouse had completely disappeared. In the 1990s work at the Trafford Park factory was transferred, for example the traction department went to the old Dick, Kerr works at Preston, and the turbine department to the English Electric factory at Stafford. The Trafford Park factory closed completely in 1997. Despite local opposition the factory buildings were demolished in 2002 as part of the regeneration of Trafford Park. Where the large factories and docks were there are now only light commercial operations, the Lowry Centre, the Imperial War Museum North and the Trafford Centre. The only sign that British Westinghouse ever had its major factory here is the street still bearing the name Westinghouse Road.

Metropolitan-Vickers Electrical Company Limited

39612

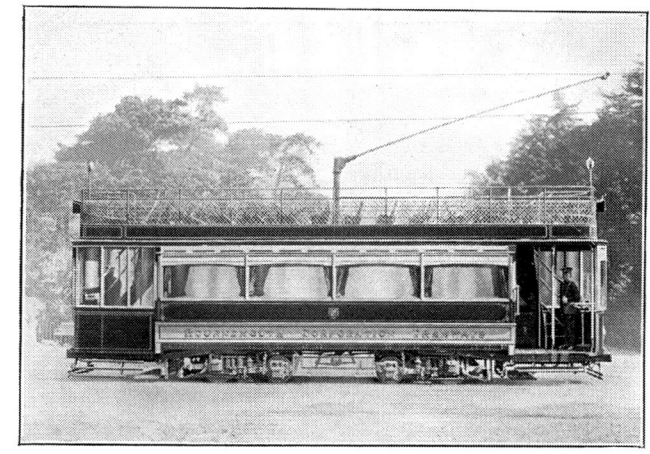

Fig. 4.—One of over 170 Bournemouth Corporation Tramway Cars fitted with Metropolitan-Vickers Magnetic Brake Equipments.

Bournemouth also used the magnetic brakes. (Author's collection)

Magnetic Brake Equipments

39611

Fig. 5.—One of over 200 Newcastle-on-Tyne Corporation Tramcars fitted with Metropolitan-Vickers Magnetic Brake Equipments.

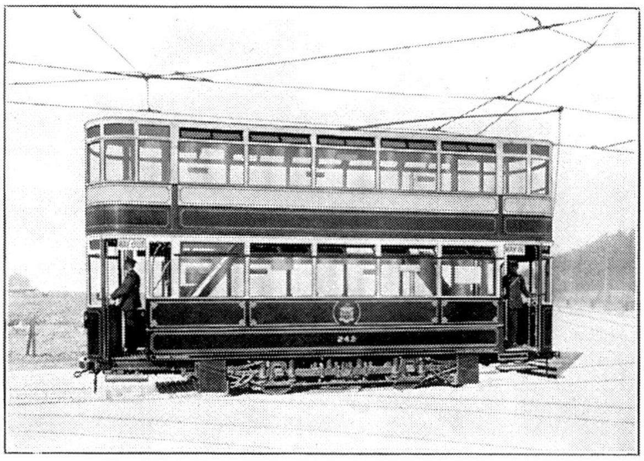

Newcastle-on-Tyne was another extensive user. (Author's collection)

12   Metropolitan-Vickers Electrical Company Limited

32803

Fig. 19.—Group of Tramcars equipped twenty years ago with **Metropolitan-Vickers Magnetic Brakes.**
All the Tramway Undertakings referred to in the above illustrations remain users of Metropolitan-Vickers Magnetic Brakes, after twenty years' experience.

3958Ch

Fig. 20.—View of the Metropolitan-Vickers Works at Trafford Park, Manchester.

591/1-1   Form No. **0558**
Published by Metropolitan-Vickers Electrical Co. Ltd., Manchester, Eng.   Printed by The Broadway Press, Dartford and London. (21999)

The final page of the booklet featuring more systems that used the Metrovick magnetic brake. (Author's collection)

These large vehicles supplied to Johannesburg each carry 105 Passengers. Electrical equipment is by AEI and the chassis by the Sunbeam Trolleybus Co. Ltd.

AEI has supplied trolleybus and tramcar equipment for many parts of the world. The above illustrates one of the more recent orders for 20 equipments for vehicles each with a laden weight of between 18 and 19 tons.

All enquiries should be addressed to the local AEI office or direct to AEI Traction Division, Trafford Park, Manchester 17.

 **Associated Electrical Industries Ltd.
Traction Division**
MANCHESTER AND LONDON

K/V001

AEI continued to make equipment for electrical road transport, but by now it was mainly for trolleybuses not tramcars. (Author's collection)

Chapter 9
THE DECLINE AND FALL OF GEORGE WESTINGHOUSE

The way in which George Westinghouse managed the financial aspects of his companies was somewhat difficult. This is illustrated by the Annual General Meetings of British Westinghouse. The first AGM was in 1901 when sales were reported as over half a million pounds. However, the profit was £10,000, just 2% of sales. This was understandable for a new company, but the next year the profit was £50,000 on an income of three quarters of a million pounds and the dividend 7%. By the third year the turnover was nearly £1 million and the dividend was again 7%. In the fourth year (1904) the turnover had increased to £1.5 million, but the dividend was reduced to 6%. The fifth year saw no dividend for the shareholders, much to their annoyance. The sixth year saw a loss after payment to debenture holders, loans and exceptional expenditure on the Mersey Railway meant a loss of £15,000 and again no dividend. It is very likely that the bid for the Mersey Railway (a very small line) was very much a 'loss-leader' to gain a foothold in the British railway market and to gain work for the Trafford Park factory. This brought the company to 1907, the year the American Company went into receivership. It has been suggested that the major reason for the lack of profits and dividend for British Westinghouse was that most of the profits were filtered back to the American company to pay off the capital used to build the British factory. This was done secretly so that the shareholders would not realise that they were subsidising the American concern.

In 1907 in the USA there was a national financial crisis which found the weaknesses in the Westinghouse Company's poor financial management. For nine years there had been no annual statements and no annual meetings of shareholders. A report was issued in 1906, but this added together six years of income to present an apparently healthy profit. In fact the company had been losing money for the whole period. This became evident in the autumn of 1906 and the value of its shares fell. In 1907 the company went into receivership. In addition the company had agreements with Tesla regarding his AC current patents. The American company was unable to honour the royalty payments. In order to save the company George Westinghouse had to rescind the original royalty agreements and Tesla was paid $216,000 as an outright

George Westinghouse in his latter years photographed appearing still at work, but by this time he had been ousted from his major companies. (Author's collection)

His service in the American civil war entitled George Westinghouse to be buried in the Arlington National Cemetery, joined later by his wife Marguerite. (Author's collection)

In 1930 his employees raised funds for a memorial, sculpted by Daniel Chester French, that was erected in Schenley Park, Pittsburgh. (Author's collection)

tions. Soon after his rejection by his largest company his health started to fail. Relationships with the new management of the largest company were clearly very difficult. The British company was going its own way, leading to the company severing its financial connections with the American company in 1918. So his difficulties were getting more rather than less. His health declined and he died in New York on 12 March 1914.

One would expect that the British tramway trade press would have recognised the contribution made to the development of tramways, particularly in the design of more powerful motors and the safety of the Newell-Westinghouse brake, and that his obituary would appear in every magazine. Not so. Without exception his death was totally ignored by all the tramway magazines in this country. This must surely be the final snub to an American who never gained anything but the most grudging acceptance by the British tramway establishment.

The work of the American Westinghouse Electric Corporation continued and it is now one of the world's largest suppliers of equipment and services relating to the control, distribution, generation and use of electric power, and is also the leading producer of nuclear power reactors. It also supplied most of the reactors for the United States Navy's nuclear-powered submarines and surface ships. It also owns a subsidiary that has 13 radio stations and five commercial television stations in the USA.

purchase of all the patents (worth around $12 million in today's money). George Westinghouse held on as President, but lost his executive power. However, it was clear that things were far from well as the board had to twice send him on six month 'vacations'. By 1911 the board felt enough was enough and he was voted out of office.

He was now 64 – in his career he had created over 50 companies and had been President of 30 corpora-

As an American civil war veteran George Westinghouse was entitled to be buried in the Arlington National Cemetery. This was carried out and he now lies with his wife Marguerite under a large stone memorial. Although rejected by the new management George Westinghouse was always admired by his workforce. In 1930 his employees raised funds for a memorial, sculpted by Daniel Chester French, that was erected in Schenley Park, Pittsburgh. There is also a George Westinghouse Museum in Wilmerding, Pennsylvania that celebrates his life and works. The museum is in the Castle, Commerce Street, a building that was once the general offices of the Westinghouse Air Brake Company.

In Britain the name Westinghouse is mostly associated with railway braking, and all train passengers owe a debt of gratitude to George Westinghouse for making rail travel far safer for everyone. But in tramway circles he will also be remembered with affection for the developments in controllers, motors and braking that contributed considerably to the modernisation of tramcar design.

A more detailed view of the memorial in Schenley Park. (Author's collection)

Though not part of Metropolitan Vickers, a company that no longer had his name, George Westinghouse could be satisfied that it continued to produce electrical equipment for Britain's tramways and industries as this brochure shows. (Tramway and Light Railway Society Archive).

More tramcars with Westinghouse or Metrovick equipment
All pictures courtesy of Tramway and Light Railway Society Archive

Aberdeen Corporation Tramways.

Cheltenham & District Light Railway.

Belfast Corporation Tramways.

Croydon Corporation Tramways.

Brighton Corporation Tramways.

Bournemouth Corporation Tramways.

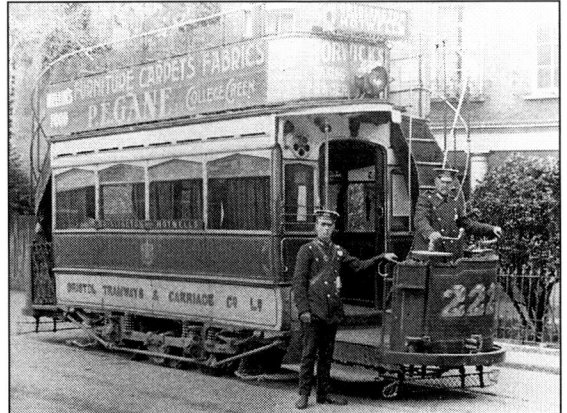
Bristol Tramways & Carriage Co.

Halifax Corporation Tramways.

Ipswich Corporation Tramways.

Huddersfield Corporation Tramways.

Leyton UDC Tramways.

Portsdown & Horndean Light Railway.

Appendix 1
COMPANIES ESTABLISHED BY GEORGE WESTINGHOUSE

1869
Westinghouse Air Brake Company

1870-1880
Compagnie Des Freins Westinghouse
Westinghouse European Brake Company

1880-1890
American Brake Company
Consolidated Electric Light Company
East Pittsburgh Improvement Company
Fuel Gas and Electric Engineering Company
Philadelphia Company
Sawyer-Man Electric Company
Union Switch and Signal Company
United Electric Light and Power Company
Westinghouse Brake Company Limited
Westinghouse Bremsen Gesellschaft
Westinghouse Company [Schenectady]
Westinghouse Electric and Manufacturing Company
Westinghouse Electric Company
Westinghouse Electric Company, Limited [London]
Westinghouse Foundry Company
Westinghouse Machine Company
Westinghouse, Church, Kerr and Company

1890-1900
British Westinghouse Electric and Manufacturing Company
Bryant Electric Company
Electro-Magnetic Traction Company
Emery Pneumatic Lubricator Company
French Westinghouse Electric Company
Manhattan General Construction Company
Perkins Electric Switch Manufacturing Company
Pittsburgh Meter Company
R.D. Nuttall Company
Security Investment Company
SociétéAnonyme Westinghouse [Russia]
Standard Car Heating and Ventilating Company
Standard Underground Cable Company
Walker Electric Company
Waterhouse Electric Company
Westinghouse Glass Company
World's Fair Equipment Company

1900-1910
Bergmann Electric Werke, A.G.
Canadian Westinghouse Company, Limited
Compagnie Internationale Pr. Le Chauffage Des Chemins De Fer Systeme Heintz, Limited
Clyde Valley Electric Power Company, Limited
Cooper Hewitt Electric Company
Laurentide Mica Company, Limited
McCandless Lamp Company
McKenzie-Holland and Westinghouse Power Signal Company
Milwaukee Locomotive Manufacturing Company
National Brake and Electric Company
Nernst Lamp Company
Pittsburgh High Voltage Insulator Company
Società Italiana Westinghouse
Société Anonyme Pr. L'Exploitation Des Procédés Westinghouse Leblanc
Société Anonyme Westinghouse [France]
Société Électrique Westinghouse De Russie
Société Hongroise D'Auto Système Westinghouse
Traction and Power Securities Company
Trafford Real Estate Company
Trafford Water Company
United Pump and Power Company
Westinghouse Automatic Air and Steam Coupler Company
Westinghouse Brake Company, Ltd [Australasia]
Westinghouse Cooper Hewitt Company, Ltd
Westinghouse Elektricitaets-Gesellschaft mbh
Westinghouse Friction Draft Gear Company
Westinghouse Interworks Railway Company
Westinghouse Lamp Company
Westinghouse Metal Filament Lamp Company
Westinghouse Metallfaden Glühlampenfabrik Gesellschaft
Westinghouse Patent Bureau [London]
Westinghouse Traction Brake Company

1910-1914
Canadian Concrete Products Company, Ltd
Comp. Pour Les Applications Des Rayons Ultra-Violet [France]
Compagnie Des Lampes À Filaments Métalliques
Copeland Electric Stove Company
Electric Properties Corporation
Fountain Electrical Floor Box Corporation
Krantz Manufacturing Company, Inc
Locomotive Stoker Company
National Steel Foundries
New England Westinghouse Company
Page-Storm Drop Forge Company
Soc. Int. Pour Les Applications Des Rayons Ultra-Violet [Belgium]
Westinghouse Air Spring Company
Westinghouse Electric Export Company
Westinghouse Gear and Dynamometer Company
Westinghouse Norsk Elekrisk Artienselskap
Westinghouse Pacific Coast Brake Company

Appendix 2
SURVIVING WESTINGHOUSE AND METROVICK CONTROLLERS

WESTINGHOUSE

TRAMCAR	CONTROLLER	LOCATION	NOTES
Belfast no. 249	200	Ulster Folk and Transport Museum	Original controllers
Bournemouth no. 85	T1C	Museum of Electricity, Christchurch	Original controllers
Chesterfield Corporation no. 7	T2C	Crich Tramway Village	Controllers are replacements, originals lost
Douglas Head Marine Drive no. 1	28A	Crich Tramway Village	Original 1896 controllers, believed to be the earliest surviving Westinghouse controllers in Britain
London County Council no. 106	T2A	Crich Tramway Village	The tram was originally fitted with Dick, Kerr DB1 controllers, the Westinghouse controller being fitted in 1924
London Transport no. 1622	T2C	Crich Tramway Village	Controllers are replacements, originals lost
West Ham no. 102 (LT 290)	T2C	London Transport Museum, Covent Garden	Original controllers

METROVICK

TRAMCAR	CONTROLLER	LOCATION	NOTES
Glasgow Corporation no. 22	OK26B	Crich Tramway Village	
Glasgow Corporation no. 812	OK26B	Crich Tramway Village	
Glasgow Corporation no. 1089	OK26B	Glasgow Museum of Transport, Kelvin Hall	
Glasgow Corporation no. 1297	Electro-pneumatic	Crich Tramway Village	
Glasgow Corporation no. 1392	Electro-pneumatic	Glasgow Museum of Transport, Kelvin Hall	
Leeds number 600	Electro-pneumatic	Crich Tramway Village	
Liverpool Corporation no. 869	Electro-pneumatic	Crich Tramway Village	
London County Council no. 1	OK34B	Crich Tramway Village	Fitted with air brake controller
London Transport no.1858	OK29B	East Anglia Museum of Transport, Carlton Colville	

The 1896 controller on the Douglas Southern Tramway car no. 1 was made in the USA. The tram is preserved at Crich Tramway Village. Note both handles are removable. (Author)

The controller on Bournemouth number 85 dates back to 1914 and can be seen on the tramcar at the Museum of Electricity, Christchurch. (Author)

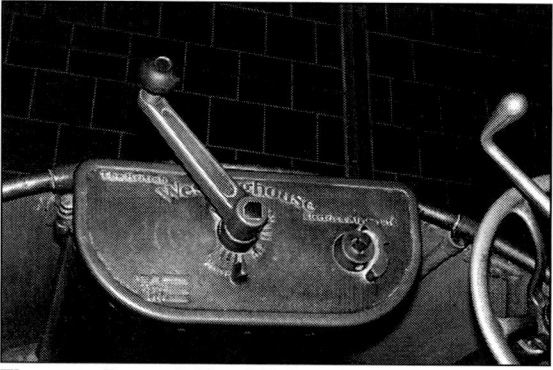

The controller on Belfast 249 dates back to 1906 and was probably made in Manchester. The tramcar is preserved in the Ulster Folk and Transport Museum. (Author)

London County Council no. 106 when built was fitted with a Dick, Kerr DB1 controller. The Westinghouse T2A controller was fitted in 1924. (Author)

This front photograph of LCC 106 shows the prominent height of the Westinghouse controller. (Author)

The controllers on the preserved tramcar Chesterfield no. 7 are not original, but are British Westinghouse products. The tram can be seen at Crich Tramway Village. (Author)

London Transport tramcar no. 1 is preserved at Crich Tramway Village and has its original OK34B controllers. Note the box on the top is the air brake attachment. (Author)

The Westinghouse controllers on London tramcar no. 1622 are replacements. The tram is preserved at Crich Tramway Village. (Author)

The London tramcar no. 1858 can be seen at the East Anglia Museum of Transport with its original Metropolitan Vickers controllers. (Author)

Another view of the controller on LCC 106. (Author)

Appendix 3

TYPES OF MOTORS PRODUCED BY BRITISH WESTINGHOUSE AND METROPOLITAN VICKERS

BRITISH WESTINGHOUSE

SERIES	HP	NOTES
12	25	First totally enclosed motor and gear box. Introduced c.1895
12A	25	A little lighter than the 12. Introduced c.1895
38	50	Included 38A and 38B variations. Introduced c.1899
46	25	Introduced c.1897
49	30/35	Introduced c. 1900
56		
80	40	
90		Introduced c. 1907
200	30/35	A disadvantage of the motor was that the bottom clearance with 30-inch wheels was just 2 inches. This did not allow for the full life to be obtained from the tyres. In practice slightly larger wheels (31.75 inches) were usually fitted.
220	40	
225	35	Introduced c.1919
307		
323	45	

METROVICK

SERIES	HP	NOTES
MV101	60	Trams with 24 to 29 inch wheel diameter, standard gauge
MV101A	40	Trams with 24 to 29 inch wheel diameter, standard gauge
MV101AR	40	Trams with 24 to 29 inch wheel diameter, standard gauge
MV101AX	40	Trams with 24 to 29 inch wheel diameter, standard gauge
MV101B	50	Trams with 24 to 29 inch wheel diameter, standard gauge
MV101BR	50	Trams with 24 to 29 inch wheel diameter, standard gauge
MV101D	60	Trams with 24 to 29 inch wheel diameter, standard gauge
MV101DR	60	Trams with 24 to 29 inch wheel diameter, standard gauge
MV102	50	Trams with 30 to 35 inch wheel diameter, standard gauge
MV102C	50	Trams with 30 to 35 inch wheel diameter, standard gauge
MV102D	60	Trams with 30 to 35 inch wheel diameter, standard gauge
MV102X	50	Trams with 30 to 35 inch wheel diameter, with roller bearings, standard gauge
MV104	50	Trams with 30 to 35 inch wheel diameter, standard gauge
MV104Y	50	Trams with 30 to 35 inch wheel diameter, standard gauge
MV105	42	Trams with 24 to 29 inch wheel diameter, metre gauge
MV105B	50	Trams with 24 to 29 inch wheel diameter, metre gauge
MV105S	42	Trams with 30 to 35 inch wheel diameter, standard gauge
MV105BS	50	Trams with 30 to 35 inch wheel diameter, standard gauge
MV105W	42	Trams with 24 to 29 inch wheel diameter, metre gauge
MV105BW	50	Trams with 24 to 29 inch wheel diameter, 3 feet or metre gauge
MV105BZ	50	Trams with 24 to 29 inch wheel diameter, standard gauge
MV106	30	
MV107		
MV109		
MV114		
MV115		
MV116		Aberdeen nos. 87-98 1920/21.45hp
MV121	40	
MV226		
MV307		
MV323		

Appendix 4
BRITISH TRAMWAY SYSTEMS USING WESTINGHOUSE/ METROVICK EQUIPMENT

All pictures courtesy of Tramway and Light Railway Society Archive

As far as can be determined the sales records of Westinghouse and Metropolitan Vickers tramway products have been lost. This table is a reconstruction of the sales using what information is available from published historical researches of tramway systems. The listing is complicated by a number of factors:

Operators often replaced the motors of their older tramcars with newer, more powerful and lighter examples, not necessarily from the original manufacturer. So tramcars may have started with Westinghouse motors, but had another company's products fitted at a later date, or vice-versa, or had the original Westinghouse motors replaced by other Westinghouse or Metropolitan Vickers motors.

In such instances a batch of motors may have been purchased and fitted by the operator to those cars needing new motors, but without keeping a record of the changes. This is apparent in the table where the car numbers are given as a number of cars, without identifying individual cars. Edinburgh was particularly prone to this.

To confuse matters more, some operators renumbered tramcars or replaced old trams with new cars but re-using the old numbers. The reader is asked to note the date of the purchase of the motors and determine what tramcar number changes may have taken place prior to that date.

The table does illustrate the mixture of different manufacturer's motors, controllers and trucks, clearly showing that manufacturers ensured that their products were entirely compatible with all other makers.

The table is as complete and as accurate as is possible with current knowledge. Please contact the author via the publisher if you are able to provide additional information.

SYSTEM & CAR NUMBERS	YEAR	MOTORS	CONTROLLERS	BODY	TRUCK(S)
Aberdare UDC					
11-20	1913	WH 200	DK DB1-K4	Brush	Peckham P22
6-9	1914	WH 200	DK DB1-K4	Brush	Peckham P22
1-5; 10; 21-26	1921	MV 323V	MV T1/C	Brush	Peckham P22
Aberdeen Corp					
1-8	1899	WH 46	WH 90	Brush	Brill 21E
9-20	1901	WH 46	WH 90	Brush	Brill 21E
21-56	1902	WH 46	WH 90	BEC	Brill 21E
57-69	1902	WH 46	WH 90	ACT	Brill 21E
68-71	1912	WH 46	WH 90M	Milnes Voss	Brill 21E
72-77	1913	Brush	WH 90M	J T Clark	Brill 21E
78-83	1914	Brush	WH 90M	Brush	M&G 21EM
84-86	1918	Brush	WH 90M	ACT	Brill 21E
66-67	1919	GE 200K	WH 90M	ACT	Brill 21E

1899 Aberdeen tramcar.

Bournemouth used Westinghouse equipment.

SYSTEM & CAR NUMBERS	YEAR	MOTORS	CONTROLLERS	BODY	TRUCK(S)
87-98	1920	WM 323	WH 90M	ACT	Brill 21E
57-61	1922	GE 200K	WH 90M	ACT	Brill 21E
62-63	1923	GE 200K	WH 90M	ACT	Brill 21E
99	1923	GE 200K	WH 90M	ACT	Brill 21E
39-52	1947	MV 105DW	EE DB1	MCTD	Peckham P35
Bath Electric Tramway Ltd					
1-26	1903	WH 49B	WH 90M	Milnes	Milnes
50-53	1903	WH 49B	WH 90M	Milnes	Milnes
27-34	1904	WH 49B	WH 90M	Milnes	Milnes
54-55	1904	WH 49B	WH 90M	Milnes	Milnes
Water Car	1903	WH 49B	WH 90M	BMR	BMR
Batley Corporation					
49-56	1903	WH 200	WH 90	BEC	Brill 21E
Belfast Corporation					
1-170	1905	WH 200	WH 90M	Brush	Brill 21E
201-250	1906	WH 200	WH 90M	BelCT	Brill 21E
171-192	1908	WH 200	WH 90M	BelCT	Brill 21E
251-291	1908	WH 200	WH 90M	BelCT	Brill 21E
342-381	1930	MV102DR	MV OK-34B	Brush	M&T
382-391	1930	MV102DR	MV OK-34B	SMW	M&T
Some of 392-441	1935	MV	MV OK-27B or MV OK-34B	SMW/EE	M&T
Blackburn Corporation					
31	1899	Siemens	WH	Milnes	Brill 22E
Blackpool & Fleetwood Tramroad Co.					
35-37	1910	WH 200	WH 90M	UEC	UEC M&G
Bolton Corporation					
87-96	1906	WH 46	WH 90M	Brush	Brill 21E
Bournemouth Corporation					
1-20	1902	WH 49B	WH 90	Milnes	Brill 22E
21-48	1902	WH 49B	WH 90	Milnes	Peckham
49-54	1904	WH 49	WH 90M	Milnes	Brill 22E
71-81	1907	WH 200	WH 90M	Brush	Brill 22E
83-92	1914	WH 226	WH T1/C	UEC	Brill 22E
113-132	1924	MV 104Y	MV T1/C	Brush	Brill 22E
Bradford Corporation					
1-16	1898	WH	WH 28A	Brush	Peckham
17-28	1899	WH	WH 28A	Brush	Peckham
Brighton Corporation					
1-25	1901	WH 30hp	?	Milnes	Peckham
26-30	1902	WH 30hp	?	Milnes	Peckham
31-40	1903	EHC	WH	Milnes	Brush A
54-55	1917	WH 30hp	?	Milnes	Brill 21E
Bristol Tramway & Carriage Co.					
203-232	1900	WH 49B	WH 90	Bristol	McGuire
Burton & Ashby					
1-13	1905	WH 80	WH 210	Brush	Brush AA
14-20	1906	WH 80	WH 210	Brush	Brush AA
Bury Corporation					
1-14	1903	WH 49B	WH 90	Milnes	McGuire MT
15-28	1903	WH 49B	WH 90	Milnes	McGuire
29-34	1904	WH 200	WH 90M	BEC	M&G
35	1905	WH 200	WH 90M	WS	M&G
36-41	1906	WH 200	WH 90M	Brush	M&G 21EM
42-47	1907	WH 49B	WH 90M	UEC	M&G 21EM
48-50	1910	WH 49B	WH 90M	UEC	M&G 21E M&G 21E
51-54	1913	WH 49B	WH 90M	UEC	M&G 21E
Water car	1906	WH 49B	WH 90M		M&G
Cardiff Corporation					

SYSTEM & CAR NUMBERS	YEAR	MOTORS	CONTROLLERS	BODY	TRUCK(S)
116-130	1904	WH	WH	Milnes	Brush MT
City of Carlisle Electric Tramway Co. Ltd					
15	1923	WH 46M	WH 210	EE	Brill 21E
Cheltenham & District Light Railway					
1-8	1901	WH 30hp	WH	Steph	Peckham
9-12	1902	WH 30hp	WH	Glouc	Peckham
21-23	1921	MV 323	WH T1/C	EE	Preston
Chesterfield Corporation					
1-12	1904	WH 25hp	WH 90M	Brush	Brush
13-14	1907	WH 25hp	WH 90M	Brush	Brush
16-18	1914	WH 25hp	WH 90M	Brush	Peckham P22
Water Car	1909	WH 25hp	WH 90M	Brush	Brush
Clontarf & Hill of Howth Tramroad Co. Ltd					
1-8	1901	WH	BTH	Brush	Brill 22E
Colne Corporation					
14-16	1926	MV 101BR	MV OK-6B	Brush	Peckham P22
Coventry Corporation					
1-4	1895	WH12	WH 28A	Brush	Peckham
5-8	1896	WH12	WH 28A	CET	Peckham
9-10	1898	WH 46	WH 28A	CET	Peckham
Nov-20	1899	WH 46	WH 28A	Brush	M&G
31-36	1907	WH 200	WH 90M	Milnes Voss	M&G
37-41	1910	WH200	DK DB1-G1	Brush	Peckham
42	1913	WH 200	DK DB1-K3	CCT	
Croydon Corporation					
36-45(II)	1906	WH 200	WH 90M	Brush	M&G 21EM
56-60(II)	1906	WH 200	WH 90M	Brush	M&G 21EM
61-70	1907	WH 200	WH 90M	Brush	Brill 21E
71-75	1911	WH 200	WH 90M	Brush	Brush 21E
Darlington Corporation					
1-16	1903	WH 46	WH 200	Milnes	McGuire
Darwen Corporation					
1-5	1900	WH	WH	Milnes	Brill 22E
15	1905	WH	Raworth WH	Milnes Voss	M&G 21E
16-17	1906	WH	Raworth WH	Milnes Voss	M&G 21E
10(II)	1933	MV	BTH 510M	DCT	Burnley
Douglas Southern Electric Tramway					
1-6	1896	WH 12A	WH 28A	Brush	Baltimore
Dublin & Blessington Steam Tramway Co.					
1-2 PE	1917	WH	?	?	MT

Edinburgh tramcar from a Metropolitan Vickers catalogue.

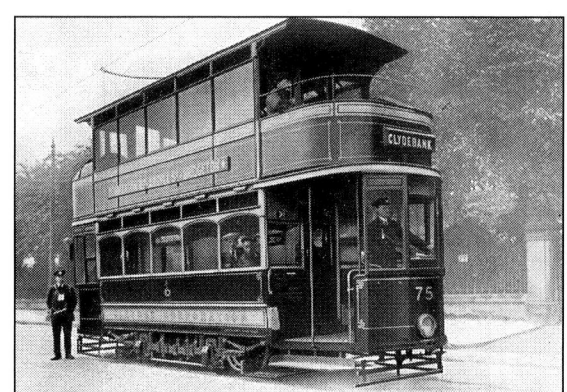

From the same catalogue is this Glasgow tramcar.

SYSTEM & CAR NUMBERS	YEAR	MOTORS	CONTROLLERS	BODY	TRUCK(S)
Dumbarton Burgh					
1-6	1907	WH 200	WH 90M	Brush	M&G 21EM
Edinburgh Corporation					
115	1922	GEC	MV OK-2B	ECT	Brill
20 cars	1922	MV 101	?	ECT	Peckham
16 cars	1923	MV 101	?	ME	Peckham
150 cars	1923	MV 101	?	ECT	Peckham
14 cars	1923	MV 101	?	LF	Peckham
14 cars	1924	MV 101	?	ECT	Peckham
270-311	1925	MV 101BR	BTHB510E	LF	Peckham
312-331	1925	MV 101BR	BTHB510E	EE	Peckham
332-336	1926	MV 101BR	BTHB510E	ECT	Peckham
40 cars	1926	MV 101BR	BTHB510E	ECT	Peckham
38 cars	1930	MV 101BR	BTHB510E	ECT	Peckham
13 cars	1931	MV 101BR	BTHB510E	ECT	Peckham
180	1932	MV 101BR	MV	ECT	EMB
250-259	1932	MV 101BR	?	PAC	M&T
260, 262	1933	MV 101BR	?	MC	M&T
261	1933	MV 101BR	?	ECT	Peckham
6 cars	1934	MV 101BR	?	MC	M&T
3 cars	1934	MV 101BR	?	EE	M&T
3 cars	1934	MV 101BR	?	HN	M&T
6 cars	1935	MV 101BR	?	EE	Peckham
6 cars	1935	MV 101BR	?	MC	M&T
8 cars	1935	MV 101BR	?	HN	Peckham
46 cars	1937	MV 101BR	?	ECT	Peckham
38 cars	1938-50	MV 101BR	?	ECT	Peckham
Erith UDC					
1-14	1905	WH 49B	WH 90	Brush	M&G 21E
15-16	1906	WH 49B	Raworth WH	Milnes Voss	M&G
Water car	1905	WH	WH 90	M&G	M&G
Farnworth UDC					
1-8	1901	WH 49B	WH 90	Milnes	Brill 22E
9-13	1902	WH 49B	WH 90	Milnes	Brill 22E
Glasgow Corporation					
1	1899	WH 49B	WH 210	GCT	Brill 21E
2-22	1901	WH 49M	WH 210	GCT	Brill 21E
17 cars	1902	WH 49M	WH 210	GCT	Brill 21E
13 cars	1903	WH 49M	WH 210	GCT	Brill 21E
441 cars	1899-1910	WH 49B	WH 90	GCT/Glouc	Brill 21E
901-980	1900	WH 49B	WH 90	GCT	Brill 21E
123 cars	1904	WH 49B	WH 90	GCT	Brill 21E
101 cars	1906	WH 49B	WH 90	GCT	Brill 21E/M&G 21E
20 cars	1909	WH 49B	WH	GCT	Brill/M&G
312 cars	1910	WH 49B	WH	GCT	Brill/Brush
1089	1926	BTH 264	MV T4A	GCT	Brill 77 E1
24 cars	1928	MV101DR	MV	HN/RYP/GCT/Brush	HN MT
1141-1142	1936	MV109AW	MV 109AW	GCT	M&T
1293-1392	1949	MV109AR	MV	GCT	M&T
7 cars	1954	GEC	MV	GCT	M&T
Works cars	1907	WH 49B	WH	GCT	Brill 21E
Greenock & Port Glasgow					
40	1908	WH	Raworth	UEC	Brill 21E
Halifax Corporation					
11-14	1898	WH 200	WH	Milnes	Peckham
15-32	1899	WH 200	WH	Milnes	Peckham
33-58	1900	WH 200	WH	Milnes	Peckham
59-70	1901	WH 200	WH	Brush	Brush 21E
71-82	1902	WH 200	WH	Brush	Brush 21E
83-94	1903	WH 200	WH	Brush	Brush 21E

SYSTEM & CAR NUMBERS	YEAR	MOTORS	CONTROLLERS	BODY	TRUCK(S)
13 cars	1921	MV 307VB	EE DB1-K3	HCT	?
103-106	1924	MV 307	EE DB1-K3	HCT	?
Huddersfield Corporation					
26-31	1901	WH 80	WH 90	BEC	BEC SB60
32-50	1902	WH 80	WH 90	BEC	BEC SB60
68-70	1903	WH 80	WH 90	BEC	BEC SB60
71-72	1904	WH 80	WH 210	Milnes Voss	Brush
Hull Corporation					
16-25	1899	WH46	WH 90	Milnes	Brill 21E
26-30	1899	WH	WH 90	Brill	Brill 21E
31-60	1900	WH	WH 90	Brush	Brill 21E
61-65	1900	WH	WH 90	ER&TCW	Brill 21E
101	1900	WH	WH 90	Milnes	Brill 21E
102-116	1903	WH	WH	Milnes	Brill 21E
2 Water cars	1899	WH	WH	Brill	Brill 21E
Ilkeston Corporation					
10-13	1903	WH 46M	WH 210	Milnes	Brill 21E
Ipswich Corporation					
1-26	1903	WH	WH	Brush	Brush AA
27-36	1904	WH	WH	Brush	Brush AA
Works car	1904	WH	WH	Brush	Brush A
Lancashire Light Railways					
42-43	1902	WH 46	WH 90	BEC	BEC SB60
Lancaster Corporation					
1-10	1902	WH	WH	Lancaster	Brill 21
11-Dec	1905	WH	WH	Milnes Voss	M&G 21EM
Leamington & Warwick Electrical Co. Ltd					
14	1921	MV 323	WH T1/C	EE	Preston
Leeds Corporation					
411-445	1926	MV 114	MV OK9B	LCT	EMB
36 cars	1926	MV 114	MV OK9B	Brush	EMB
76-150	1926	MV 114	MV OK9B	EE	EMB
406-410	1928	MV 114	MV OK9B	LCT	EMB
255	1933	MV 109	MV OK9B	Brush	M&T
104 (II)	1943	MV 114	BTH	LCT	Peckham
601 (II)	1953	MV 109CZ	MV EP	Roe	EMB
Leyton UDC					
11-50	1906	WH 200	WH 90M	Milnes Voss	M&G
51-70	1907	WH 200	WH 90M	Milnes Voss	M&G
161-210	1931	BTH	BTH/MV OK38B	EE	EMG
Lincoln Corporation					
1-8	1905	WH 46M	WH	Brush	Brush
Liverpool & Prescot Light Railway					
42-43	1902	WH 46	WH 90	BEC	BEC SB60
Liverpool Corporation					
459-463	1899	WH 49B	WH	Brush	Peckham

Llandudno tramcar.

London E/1 car also from the catalogue.

SYSTEM & CAR NUMBERS	YEAR	MOTORS	CONTROLLERS	BODY	TRUCK(S)
1-4	1907	WH 200	WH 90	LivCT	Brill 21E
484-491	1907	WH 200	WH 90	LivCT	Brill 21E
492-500	1907	WH 200 MV104	WH 90	LivCT	Brill 21E
118	1923	MV104	K3	LivCT	STD
99	1928	MV104	K33	LivCT	STD
94, 107	1929	MV104	K33	LivCT	STD
4 cars	1929	MV104	K33	LivCT	EMB/STD
3 cars	1929	MV104	K33	LivCT	EMB
7 cars	1930	MV116	K33	LivCT	EMB/STD
2 cars	1930	MV104	K33	LivCT	EMB
1, 6 & 144	1931	MV104	K3	LivCT	STD
2 cars	1931	MV116	K33	LivCT	STD
8 cars	1931	MV116	K33	LivCT	EMB/STD
12 cars	1932	GEC	K33	LivCT	EMB
868-992	1936	GEC	MV HW	LivCT	EMB
151-188	1937	MV 116AS	MV AN	LivCT	EMB
201-300	1937	MV 116	K3	LivCT	EMB
745-756	1937		K3	LivCT	EMB
Llandudno & Colwyn Bay					
6	1914	GE 249A	WH T1C	UEC	Brill 22E
7-8	1921	GE 249A	MV T1C	Brush	Brill 22E
14-15	1921	GE 249A	MV T1C	Brush	Brill 22E
London County Council					
202-301	1904	WH 200	WH 90M	Brush	Brill 21E
302-376	1904	WH 200	WH	Brush	McGuire
377-401	1904	WH 200	WH	BEC	McGuire
402-426	1905	WH 200	WH 90M	HN	M&G
427-551	1906	WH 200	WH T2A	HN	M&G
568-601	1906	WH 200	WH T2A	Brush	M&G
602-751	1906	WH 220	WH T2A	HN	M&G
752-1001	1907	WH 220	WH T2A	HN	M&G
1002-1051	1907/8	WH 220	WH T2C	LCC	HN
1052-1226	1908/9	WH 220	WH T2C	HN	HN
1227-1426	1910	WH 220	WH T2C	HN	HF
1427	1910	WH 220	WH T2C	LCC	HN
1428-1476	1910	WH 220	WH T2C	HN	HN
1477-1676	1911/2	WH 220	WH T2C	Brush	HF
1677-1726	1910	WH 220	WH T2C	Brush	HF
1727-1776	1922	MV 121	WH T2C	HN	HN
1852-1853	1929	MV 109Z	MV OK29B	LCC	HN
552-601	1930	WH 220	WH T2C	EE	EMB
1854-1903	1930	MV 109Z	MV OK29B	EE	EMB
101-159	1931	MV 109Z	MV OK37B	HN	EMB
161-210	1931	BTH116AY	MV OK38B	EE	EMB
1	1932	MV 109Z	MV OK37B	LCC	EMB
2	1933	MV121A	MVOK47B	LCC	HN
01-04	1905	WH 200	WH 90M	M&G	M&G 21E
05-06	1908	WH 200	WH 90M	LCC	M&G 21E
013-014	1923	WH 200	WH T2A/C	LCC	Brill 22E
15	1930	WH 220	WH T2A/C	LCC	Brill 21E
016-036	1926	WH 220	WH T2A/C	LCC	Brill 21E
037-054	1930	WH 220	WH T2A/C	LCC	Brill 21E
London Transport					
1	1932	MV 109Z	MVOK 37B	LCC	EMB
2	1933	MV 121A	MVOK 47B	LCC	HN
101-131	1931	MV 109Z	MVOK 29B	HN	EMB
132-159	1931	MV 109Z	MVOK 37B	HN	EMB
162	1931	MV 121A	MVOK 4B	EE	EMB
165-166	1931	MV 121A	MVOK 4B	EE	EMB
211-294	Various	GE 200K	MVT 2G	Various	Various
331-333	1927	MV 121A	MVOK 4B	W Ham	HN

SYSTEM & CAR NUMBERS	YEAR	MOTORS	CONTROLLERS	BODY	TRUCK(S)
334-343	1927	MV 121A	MVOK 4B	Brush	HN
345-349	1911	WH 200	WH T1C	Brush	Brush 21E
350-364	1906	WH 200	WH 90	Brush	Brill 21E
402-446	1905	WH 220	WH T2A/C	HN	M&G
447	1905	GE 203N	WH T2A/C	HN	M&G
448-510	1905	WH 220	WH T2A/C	HN	M&G
512-551	1905	WH 220	WH T2A/C	HN	M&G
552-556, 558, 561, 566, 572-573, 583-584.	1929	WH 220	WH T2C	EE	M&G
557, 562-565, 570-571, 575-576, 580-582, 601.	1929	EE 301	WH T2C	EE	M&G
557, 562-565, 570-571, 575-576, 580-582, 601. 559-560, 574, 577-578, 598.	1929	MV 121A	MVOK 4B	EE	M&G
579	1929	EEDK	EECDBFm1	EE	M&G
585-587, 589-591, 594- 595, 599-600.	1930	WH 220	WH T2C	EE	M&G
588, 597, 598	1930	WH 220	WH T2C	EE	M&G
592-593	1930	MV 121A	MVOK4B	EE	M&G
596	1930	MV 121A	EECDB2	EE	M&G
602-629, 631-780	1906	WH 220	WH T2A/C	HN	M&G
630	1906	CP Std	WH T2C	HN	M&G
781	1907	GEWT293A	WH T2C	HN	M&G
782	1907	A	EECDB2F	HN	M&G
784	1907	MV114CR	BTH B519A	HN	M&G
785	1907	CP C150B	BTH 510	HN	M&G
786	1907	EE 301A	WH T2C	HN	M&G
787	1907	GEC201A	WH T2C	HN	M&G
788	1907	150B5		HN	M&G
789-791, 793-800, 804- 805, 807, 809-813, 815, 823, 824-832, 834-836, 838-839, 940, 947-948.	1907	EE 301	WH T2C	HN	M&G

Lowestoft tramcar with its smart crew posing for the photographer.

Another Lowestoft car that for some reason has a damaged gate, but more interestingly the controller has been opened.

SYSTEM & CAR NUMBERS	YEAR	MOTORS	CONTROLLERS	BODY	TRUCK(S)
792, 801, 806, 817-820, 822, 840, 852-932, 934- 936, 938-939, 941-946, 949-951, 997-999, 1001r, 1043-1048.	1907	WH 220	WH T2C	HN	M&G
1000	1907	MV 121A	WH T2C	HN	M&G
1003, 1042	1907	EE 301	WH T2C	HN	M&G
1009, 1032	1907	EEDK31C	MVOK4B	LCC	M&G
1034-1041	1907	MV 121A	EECDB2C	LCC	M&G
808, 1049-1051	1907	MV 121A	MVOK4B	LCC	M&G
1052-1058, 1063-1074, 1102, 1104-1108, 1110- 1114, 1117-1136, 1147- 1162, 1164-1170, 1180, 1183-1186, 1188-1189, 1192-1194, 1196-1203, 1209-1210, 1217, 1221.	1908	WH 220	WH T2C	HN	HF
1059-1061, 1077-1099, 1101, 1103, 1137-1146, 1163, 1171-1179, 1181-1182, 1211-1214, 1220, 1222-1226.	1908	MV 121A	MVOK4B	HN	HF
1187, 1190-1191	1908	EE 301A	MVOK4B	HN	HF
1195, 1204, 1208, 1215- 1216, 1218-1219.	1908	EEDK31C	WH T2C	HN	HF
1205-1207	1908	WH 220	EECDB2C	HN	HF
1228-1246, 1248-1251, 1255, 1267, 1288, 1293, 1316, 1322, 1351-1369, 1371-1394, 1396-1415, 1419-1426.	1909	MV 121A	MVOK4B	HN	HN
1253-1254, 1256-1266, 1268-1272, 1274, 1276, 1278-1287, 1289-1290, 1292, 1294-1305, 1307- 1309, 1311, 1313-1315. 1318-1321, 1323-1342, 1344-1349, 1416-1417.	1909	WH 220	WH T2C	HN	HN
1273, 1317, 1395	1909	EEDK31C	MVOK4B	HN	HN
1275, 1291, 1310, 1370	1909	EE301	WH T2C	HN	HN
1418	1909	MV 116DY	EECDB2K	HN	HN
802	1910	MV 121A	MVOK4B	HN	M&G
803, 814, 816, 821, 833, 837.	1910	EE 301	WH T2C	HN	M&G
1427	1910	WH 220	WH T2C	LCC	HN
1428-1440, 1442-1443, 1445, 1447-1514.	1910	WH 220	WH T3C	HN	HN
1441	1910	MV 121A	EEDB1K	LCC	HN
1444	1910	MV 121A	MV T2C	LCC	HN
1446	1910	MV 121A	MVOK4B	LCC	HN
1583, 1606, 1608, 1610, 1612-1614, 1617-1618, 1621, 1624, 1626, 1636, 1640, 1644-1646.	1910	EE 301	WH T2C	Brush	HF
1584-1587,1605, 1607, 1609, 1611, 1615-1618, 1620, 1622, 1625,					

Manchester tramcar with an early Westinghouse controller.

Mansfield had Westinghouse controllers, built in 1905.

SYSTEM & CAR NUMBERS	YEAR	MOTORS	CONTROLLERS	BODY	TRUCK(S)
1632-1635, 1637, 1639, 1641, 1649, 1677-1726.	1910	WH 220	WH T2C	Brush	HF
1588	1910	MV 121A	WH T2C	Brush	HF
1619, 1676	1910	BTH509C	WH T2C	Brush	HF
1727-1749, 1751-1776	1922	MV 121	MV T2C	HN	HN
1750	1922	MV 121	WH T2G	HN	HN
1852	1929	MV 105	MVOK4B	LCC	HN
1853	1929	MV 105	MVOK29B	LCC	HN
2166	1929	MV 105	MVOK37B	UCC	MET
1854-1897, 1899-1903	1930	MV 109	MVOK29B	EE	EMB
1898	1930	MV109Z	MVOK37B	EE	EMB
1986	1930	EE 301	MVOK4B	HN	EMB
2253	1926	MV 124	WH T2C	MET	Brush
2255	1927	MV 101DR	BTH B18	MET	Brush
2318-2357	1906	WH T2G	WH 90M	UEC Co	Brill 22E
2358-2363, 2368-2402	1902	WH 49B	WH 90M	Milnes	Brill 22E
2364-2367	1902	WH 49B	WH 90M	BEC	Brill 22E
2411	1901	MV 104	WH 90M	Milnes	Brill 22E
2466	1904	MV 104	MVOK4B	Brush	Brush
2522-2530.	1902	MV 104	WH 90M	Milnes	Brill
London United Tramway					
101-150	1901	WH 49B	WH 90	Milnes	McGuire
151-211	1902	WH 49B	WH 90	Milnes	Brill 22E
212-236	1902	BTH GE58	WH 90	BEC	Brill 22E
237-300	1902	WH 49B	WH 90	Milnes	Brill 22E
301-340	1906	WH 80/200	WH 90	UEC	Brill 22E
350	1928	MV 101	BTH	LGOC	Brush M&G
Lowestoft Corporation					
1-11	1903	WH46	WH 90	Milnes	Milnes
21-24	1903	WH46	WH 90	Milnes	Milnes MT
Dec-15	1904	WH46	WH 90	Milnes	Milnes
Works car	1903	WH	WH	BMR	Brush
Maidstone Corporation					
18	1909	WH	WH T1/R	UEC	M&G 21E
Manchester Corporation					
103	1899	WH	WH	Brush	Brill 22E
106	1899	WH	WH	Milnes	Peckham
549-648	1904	WH 200	WH 90M	Brush	Brill 22E
649-668	1907	WH 200	BTH B18	UEC	Brill 22E
748-762	1913	WH 220	BTH B18	MCTD	Brill 22E
763-767	1914	WH 225	DK DB1-K4	MCTD	Brill 22E
768-792	1919	WH 220	BTH B18	MCTD	Brill 22E
38 cars (40 sets)	1930	MV 105DW	BTH B510		
Mansfield & District					
1-12	1905	WH 200	WH 90M	HN	HN 21E

Newcastle tramcar from the Metropolitan Vickers catalogue.

Trams in Newport.

SYSTEM & CAR NUMBERS	YEAR	MOTORS	CONTROLLERS	BODY	TRUCK(S)
13-18	1906	WH 200	WH 90M	Brush	Brush AA
Metropolitan Electric Tramway					
318	1926	MV 101	BTH	MET	Brush M&G
320	1929	MV 105	EE	UCC	MET
319,321-329, 332-375	1931	BTH 509P	MV OK33B	UCC	EM
Mexborough & Swinton Tramways Co.					
17-20	1908	BTH GE58	WH 90M	Brush	Brush 21E
Middlesbrough, Stockton & Thornaby					
51-60	1901	WH 46	WH 90	Milnes	McGuire
P/W car	1907	WH 46	WH 90	IT	McGuire
Nelson Corporation					
7-9	1925	MV 104	MV T1/D	Brush	Brush 21E
Newcastle Corporation					
131-165	1901	WH 25hp	WH	Brush	Brill 21E
225-229	1914	WH 80	K3	NCT	Brill 21E
285-309	1924	WH	WH	BEC	BEC SB60
Water car	1902	MV 307VB	MV OK1B	Brush	Peckham P22
Newport Corporation					
1-30	1903	WH 30hp	WH 90	Milnes	Peckham
New St Helens District Tramways Co.					
17-36	1899	WH 46	WH 90	Brush	?
Norwich Electric Tramway					
1-40	1899	WH 46	WH 28A	Brush	Peckham
5 cars (rm)	1906	WH 28A	WH 28A	Brush	M&G
10 cars	1924	WH46	EE	EE	Peckham
6 cars	1925	WH46	EE	EE	Peckham
4 cars	1927	WH46	EE	EE	Peckham
4 cars	1928	WH46	EE	EE	Peckham
4 cars	1929	WH46	EE	EE	Peckham
4 cars	1930	WH46	EE	EE	Peckham
Water car	1900	WH	WH	Brush	Peckham
Nottingham Corporation					
58-67	1901	WH30hp	BTH	Milnes	Brill 21E
68-77	1902	WH30hp	BTH	Milnes	Brill 21E
Perth Corporation					
1-9	1905	WH	WH	Hurst Nelson	Hurst Nelson
10-Dec	1905	WH	WH	Hurst Nelson	Hurst Nelson
Plymouth Corporation					
1-6	1899	WH 46	WH	Milnes	Peckham
7-20	1901	WH 46	WH	Brush	Peckham
21-30	1902	WH 46	WH	Brush	Peckham
31-36	1905	WH	WH	Brush	Brush
37-42	1906	WH	WH T1C	Brush	Brush
43-54	1915	WH 221	WH T1C	Brush	Peckham
55-62	1916	WH 221	WH T1C	Brush	Peckham
90, 92	1919	BTH	WH T1C	Brush	Peckham
Portsdown & Horndean Light Railway					
1-14	1903	WH 200	WH 90M	BEC	BEC SB60
Rawtenstall Corporation					
1-16	1909	WH 220	WH T1/R	UEC	Preston 21E
25-32	1921	MV 307/323	MV T1	Brush	Brush
Reading Corporation					
30 nc	1920		MV		
31-32 rm	1927	MV 102DR			
Rochdale Corporation					
60-69	1912	Brush	WH	Brush	Brush D
93	1927	MV 107	MV	RCT	Brill 21E
94	1928	MV 102DR	MV	RCT	Brill 21E

SYSTEM & CAR NUMBERS	YEAR	MOTORS	CONTROLLERS	BODY	TRUCK(S)
89 rm, nc	1929	MV 102DR	MV		
Salford Corporation					
1-100	1901	WH 46C	WH 90	Milnes	Brill 21E
101-130	1903	WH 46	WH 412	Milnes	Brill 27G
131-150	1903	WH 46	WH 412	BEC	Brill 27G
151-160	1905	WH 80	WH 210	ER&TWC	Brill 22E
163-172	1906	WH 200	WH 210	UEC	Brill 21E
177-196	1908	WH 200	WH 210/T1C	UEC	M&G 21EM
197-200	1908	WH 200	WH 210/T1C	HN	M&G 21EM
151-160 (II)	1913	WH 80	WH 210	UEC	Brill 21E
213-224	1915	WH 220/5	DK DB 1K3	Brush	Brill 26E
Water car	1905	WH	WH	ER&TCW	Brill 21E
Sheffield Corporation					
451-500	1926	MV 102D	BTH OK1B	Cravens	Peckham P22
1	1927	MV 102	BTH B510	Cravens	Peckham P22
2-3	1928	MV 102	BTH B510	SCT	Peckham P22
61-130	1930	MV 102	BTH B510	SCT	Peckham P22
131-155	1930	MV 102	BTH B510	Hill	Peckham P22
370	1930	MV 116	BTH B510	SCT	Peckham P22
156-201	1933	MV 102	BTH B510	SCT	Peckham P22
202-230	1935	MV 102	BTH B510	SCT	Peckham P22
231-242	1936	MV 102DR	BTH B510	SCT	Peckham P22
243-248	1936	MV 116	BTH B510	SCT	Peckham P22
249-303	1936	MV 102DR	BTH B510	SCT	Peckham P22
14 cars	1941	MV 102DR	BTH B510	SCT	Peckham P22
501	1946	MV101DR	BTH B510	SCT	M&T 588
502-536	1950	MV101DR	BTH B510	Roberts	M&T 588
Southampton Corporation					
12 cars	1901	WH	WH	Milnes	Brill 21E
38-49	1903	WH	WH 90	HN	Brill 21E
12 cars rm	1927	MV 101BR	MV OK9B		
6 cars rm	1928	MV 101BR	MV OK9B		
6 cars rm	1929	MV 101BR	MV OK9B		
12 cars	1930	MV 101BR	MV OK9B		
Southend Corporation					
18-22	1904	WH 25hp	WH	Milnes	Brill 22E
South Metropolitan Tramways					
21	1906	WH 200	B 18	Brush	Brill 21E
52	1906	WH 200	B 18	M&G	Brush 21E
South Shields Corporation					
1-10	1905	WH30hp	WH 210	HN	HN 21E
Nov-25	1906	WH30hp	WH 210	UEC	Preston 21E
26-35	1907	WH30hp	WH 210	UEC	Preston 21E
36-40	1914	WH200	WH T1C	Brush	Peckham P22
49	1929	WH200	DK	SSCT	Smith
Water car	1913	WH200	WH T1C	Brush	Brush

The first Norwich tramcars were fitted with controllers made in America.

A coastal tramway using Westinghouse controllers was Weston-Super-Mare.

SYSTEM & CAR NUMBERS	YEAR	MOTORS	CONTROLLERS	BODY	TRUCK(S)
Southport Tramways Co					
1	1903	Brush 800C	Raworth	Brush	Brush
Stalybridge, Hyde, Mossley & Dunkinfield Tramways & Electric Board (SHMD)					
1-40	1904	WH200	WH 90M	BEC	McGuire21EM
41-55	1905	WH200	WH 90M	HN	M&G 21EM
56-60	1907	WH220	WH 90M	HN	M&G 3L
61-64	1924	WH200	WH 90M	SHMD	Brush 21E
Works car	1905	WH200	WH 90M	M&G	M&G 21EM
Sunderland Corporation					
66-71	1906	WH 30hp	WH	Brush	M&G
Swansea Improvements & Tramways Tramroads Co.					
66-67	1911	WH220	WH T1/C	SCT	LCC type
69-74	1912	WH220	WH T1/C	SCT	LCC type
68 cars	1914	WH220	WH T1/C	Brush	LCC type
Trafford Park Estates					
5-9	1903	WHB49	WH 5915	BEC	Brill 21E
10	1903	WHB49	WH 5915	BEC	Brill 27G
11	1904	WHB49	WH 5915	BEC	Brill 21E
Tyneside Tramways & Tramroads Co. Ltd					
1-4	1902	WH 80	WH	Milnes	Brill 27G
5-18	1902	WH 80	WH	Milnes	Brill 21E
19-22	1904	WH 80	WH 210	Brush	Brill 21E
23-24	1904	WH 80	WH 412	Brush	Brill 27G
25-26	1910	WH 80	WH	UEC	Brill 21E
27	1911	WH 80	WH	UEC	Preston 21E
Tower car	1920	WH 80	WH	EE	Preston 21R
Walthamstow Corporation					
1-32	1905	WH 49	WH 90M	Brush	Brush 21E
33-38	1910	WH 200	WH 90M	HN	HN 21E
47-52	1902	BTH	WH 90	BEC	Brill 22E
Water car	1905	WH 200	WH 90M	Brush	Brush AA
West Ham					
86-100	1906	WH 200	WH T2G	Milnes Voss	M&G
101-106	1910	Brush	WH T2G	UEC	Peckham
51, 60-65	1923	BTH	WH T2G	WHCT	WHCT
107-110 rm/nc	1923	BTH	WH T2G	HN	HN LCC
Water car	1905	?	WH	M&G	M&G
Weston-super-Mare & District Electric Supply Co.					
17-18	1927	WH	WH 90M	Brush	Brill
Wigan Corporation					
27-50	1903	WH200	WH 90M	HN	HN
51-62	1904	WH200	WH 90M	DK	Brill 22E
Wolverhampton Corporation					
7-9	1902	WH	WH	Milnes	Brill 21E

NOTES

The information below is additional to the table and in some instances seems to contradict the table. For example one source only identifies Glasgow as having 25 sets of MV 101DR motors (as in the table) while another (in notes below) identifies purchases of up to 467 sets of MV 101DR motors. Until further information comes to light all available details are given in the hope that readers may be able to help untangle the information about Glasgow and the other systems.

EDINBURGH CORPORATION

Edinburgh bought 128 car sets of EE DB1-K7B controllers between May 1922 and November 1923 and 232 car sets of BTH B510 controllers between 1922 and 1928. As older cars were scrapped the new replacements were mounted on the old trucks and used the old electrical equipment. However, there is a note on a drawing of OK-35B which says "as used in Edinburgh".

GLASGOW CORPORATION
The table does not identify all the motors supplied by Metropolitan Vickers to Glasgow. It is known that MV supplied Glasgow with replacement motors for 467 trams and controllers for 440 trams. The motors were mainly MV101DR, there were also some MV101CR and MV101J. In addition BTH supplied 40 sets of 101J motors. In 1951 the stock of electrical equipment included 479 sets of MV OK23B/OK26B/OK20B controllers; 7 sets of WH323V; 481 sets of MV101DR; 98 sets of MV109AR and 2 sets of MV109AW motors.

HALIFAX CORPORATION
The 13 cars fitted with MV307VB motors in 1921 are believed to be 9, 10, 11, 17, 22, 59, 64, 71, 73, 75, 76, 80, 81.

LANCASHIRE LIGHT RAILWAYS
These two cars were part of the St Helens Corporation Fleet

LINCOLN CORPORATION
Remotored in 1909/10 with WH 200 35hp motors.

LONDON COUNTY COUNCIL
The 25 cars of the 402-551 'E' Class with WH200 motors were given WH220 motors and T2A or T2C motors later years. In 1922 200 sets of high power MV322 motors were purchased to re-equip Class E/1 cars in 1924/25, they retained their WH T1 controllers. The WH220 motors displaced were used to re-motor cars of Classes A, C, D and F and the snowbrooms and snowploughs. 149 sets of MV121A split frame motors and 51 sets of MV124 box frame motors were purchased with MV OK4B controllers.

LONDON TRANSPORT
All information is for the last electrical equipment fitted to the tramcars. The information has been taken from London Transport Tramways by E.R. Oakley and C.E. Holland.

SHEFFIELD CORPORATION
Tramcars numbers 2-35 mainly had MV102 motors, but some were delivered with MV103 (including car 3); MV116 (car 28) and GEC WT28L (cars 9, 19 and 20).
Tramcars numbers 61-130 had mainly MV102DR, but some had MV107 (cars 64, 65, 67, 68 & 69) worm drive motors; four had BTH503 (cars 66, 112, 113 & 114) and four with GE203N (cars 115-118).
The 14 cars of 1941 were supplied with stock motors and not new ones. These motors were a mix of MV102; MV102DR and GE203N.

SOUTH SHIELDS CORPORATION
Car 49 received ex-LCC motors.

SWANSEA IMPROVEMENTS AND TRAMWAYS CO.
Numbers 1-30 and 56-65 fitted sometime with WH T1/C controllers

---

SYSTEMS NOT USING WESTINGHOUSE EQUIPMENT

Aberdeen Suburban Tramway
Accrington Corporation
Aidrie & Coatbridge Tramway Co.
Ashton under Lyne Corporation
Ayr Corporation
Barking UDC
Barnsley & District Electric Traction Co. Ltd
Barrow in Furness Corporation
Bessbrook & Newry Tramway CO.
Bexley UDC
Birkenhead Corporation

Birmingham & Midland Tramways Ltd
Birmingham Corporation
City of Birmingham Tramway Co. Ltd
Birmingham District Power & District Co. Ltd
Blackpool Electric Tramway Co. Ltd
Brighton & Rottingdean Seashore Electric Tramroad Co.
Burnley Corporation
Burton Corporation
Camborne & Redruth Light Railway
Cardiff Corporation

Chatham & District Light Railway Co. Ltd
Chester Corporation
Colchester Corporation
Cork Electric Tramways & Lighting Co.
(Crosby) Liverpool Overhead Railway
Cruden Bay Hotel Tramway
Dartford UDC
Dearne District
Derby Corporation
Dewsbury Ossett & Soothill Nether Tramway
Doncaster Corporation
Dover Corporation
Dublin Southern District Tramway Co.
Dublin United Tramways Co.
Dudley Stourbridge & District Electric Traction Co. Ltd
Dundee, Broughty Ferry & District Tramway Co.
Dundee Corporation
Dunfermline & District Tramway Co.
East Ham Corporation
Exeter Corporation
Falkirk & District Tramway Co.
Felixstowe Pier
Gateshead & District Tramways Co.
Giants Causeway, Portrush & Bush Valley
Glossop Tramways
Gloucester Corporation
Gosport & Fareham Tramway Co.
Gravesend & Northfleet Electric Tramway Co. Ltd
Great Grimsby Street Tramway Co.
Great Yarmouth Corporation
(Grimsby & Immingham) British Railways
Grimsby Corporation
Guernsey Railway Co. Ltd
Hartlepools
Haslingden Corporation
Hastings Tramway Co.
Hellingley Hospital
Herne Bay Pier
Ilford Corporation
Ipswich Tramway Co.
Isle of Thanet Electric Tramways & Lighting Co. Ltd
Jarrow & District Electric Traction Co. Ltd
Keighley Corporation
Kidderminster & Stourbridge
Kilmarnock Corporation
Kinver Light Railway
Kirkcaldy Corporation
Leicester Corporation
Leith Corporation
Liverpoorl Overhead Railway (Crosby)
Llanelly & District Electric Lighting & Traction Co.
Luton Corporation
Lytham St Annes Corporation
Manx Electric Railway Co. Ltd
Merthyr Electric Traction & Lighting Co. Ltd
Mid Yorkshire Tramway Co.
Middlesborough Corporation
Middleton Electric Traction Co. Ltd
Morecombe Corporation

Musselborough & District Electric Light & Traction Co. Ltd
Neath Corporation
Northampton Corporation
Notts & Derby
Oldham, Ashton & Hyde
Oldham Corporation
Paisley District Tramway Co.
Peterborough Electric Traction Co. Ltd
Plymouth, Stonehouse & Devonport Tramway Co.
Pontypridd Udc
Poole & District Electric Traction Co. Ltd
Portsmouth Corporation
Portsmouth Street Tramways
Potteries Electric Traction Co. Ltd
Preston Corporation
Ramsgate Tunnel Railway
Rhonda Tramway Co. Ltd
Rotherham Corporation
Rothesay Tramways Co. Ltd
Roundhay Electric Tramways
St Helens Corporation
Scarborough Tramways Co.
Seaton & District Tramway
Sheerness & District Electric Power & Traction Co. Ltd
Snaefell Mountain Tramway
Southend Pier
South Lancashire Tramway Co. (they had Westinghouse equipment in the ex-Farnworth trams)
Southport Corporation
South Staffordshire Tramway Co.
Stockton & Thornaby Joint Corporation Tramways
Stockport Corporation
Sunderland District Electric Tramways Ltd
Swansea & Mumbles Railway
Swindon Corporation
Taunton Electric Traction Co. Ltd
Torquay Tramways Co. Ltd
Tynemouth & District Tramway Ltd
Volks Electric Railway
Wallasey Corporation
Walsall Corporation
Walton on the Naze Pier
Warrington Corporation
Wemyss & District Tramway Co. Ltd
Wolverhampton District Electric Tramways Ltd
Worcester Electric Traction Co. Ltd
Worcester Tramways Co.
Wrexham & District Tramway Co
York Corporation
Yorkshire (West Riding) Electric Tramway Co. Ltd
Yorkshire Woollen District Electric Tramway Co. Ltd

A Mansfield tramcar during WWI with women crew.

Plymouth tramcar.

Appropriately Salford Corporation used Westinghouse controllers as the Trafford Park factory was in their borough.

Wolverhampton had just two tramcars with Westinghouse controllers.

Staleybridge, Hyde, Mossley and Dunkinfield tramcar.

A proud crew show off their Walthamstow tramcar.

Appendix 5
WESTINGHOUSE IN FRANCE

The American owned Westinghouse Brake Company set up a French subsidiary, Société des Friens Westinghouse in 1879 to supply compressed air brake systems to railways in France. The works was located at Sevran, about 40km north west of Paris, and included a workers' housing estate which was given the name Frienville ("Brake City"). The venture was successful and the group decided to try to repeat this success in the electrical field. The group established a French Westinghouse Company in 1897 by taking over an electrical works at Graville-Sainte Honorine, near Le Havre. It also took control of the Compagnie Generale de Traction et d'Électricite, which had a controlling interest in 16 French tramway companies and held a concession for the future Paris Metro.

This group was absorbed in 1901 and took the name Société Anonyme Westinghouse, which would supply air brakes and electrical plant in France, Belgium, Holland, Italy, Switzerland, Spain and Portugal. It was placed under the control of British Westinghouse group. George Westinghouse was company president, and the managing director was a Pittsburgh-trained Swiss engineer, Albert Schmid.

However, owing to its later start up, the French Westinghouse company lost market share to the Thomson-Houston group and only paid a dividend in one year (1908). In 1909 a large loan was necessary from the American company, mainly because the French company's working capital was tied up in ventures for which it had taken payment in shares, including the Sintra tramway in Portugal. They had a contract to supply the Sintra tramway, but were given shares in the company rather than outright payment (this was not unusual). The tramway lost money and the shares were worthless. However, they took up more shares later and it is believed this was because they had the contract to supply equipment for the electric lighting for the town, which they considered profitable. In 1910 they built three benzine-electric cars for the Ooster Stoomtram (Utrecht-Zeist) with bodies by Werkspoor.

In Italy the group obtained important railway electrification contracts, a condition of which was that the equipment must be made in Italy. A factory capable of building complete locomotives was established at Vado Ligure, near Savona, by the Societa Italiana Westinghouse. It was sold in 1919 to Brown Boveri.

By 1906-10 the French tramway market had ceased to expand and the Westinghouse works at Le Havre was re-equipped to build steam turbines, pumps, condensers, refrigeration plant, gas engines and petrol electric road and rail vehicles. The principal tramway activity was the supply and retrofitting of Westinghouse-Newell magnetic track brakes. The brake factory at Freinville (whose Chief Draughtsman in 1908 was Oliver Bulleid) was enlarged to make train heating systems and electro-pneumatic signalling. There was some specialisation and contract-sharing between the British and French Westinghouse companies. By 1913, Westinghouse (France) had regained financial equilibrium, at a time when British Westinghouse was at a low ebb.

In 1914 Westinghouse USA decided to sell off its European electrical subsidiaries, retaining the patents and drawing royalties. It would also retain the profitable brake and signalling company (Compagnie des Friens Westinghouse).The works at Le Havre was placed under the control of Trafford Park and eventually of Metropolitan-Vickers, who sold it in 1920 to the Swiss company CEM. They in turn merged with the Schneider Group and traded thereafter as Le Materiel Électrique Scheider-Westinghouse.

Acknowledgements

The prime mover behind this book was the late John Price. Knowing that he would not be able to complete his series on British Tramcar Manufacturers he asked for volunteers to take on the task. The major two areas remaining were English Electric and British Westinghouse. He suggested to me to address British Westinghouse first. This was fortunate, as a history of English Electric tramway products was published during my researches into this book. I would not have been able to make a start without the advice and direct help from John.

As with any historical researches the author relies on a very large number of other people either directly or through previously published information. I would like to thank them all and in particular Roy Brook, Ted Gray, F.P. Groves, Norman Henley, Roger Monk and Geoff Tribe for all their invaluable help.

There are two others who have given enormous assistance, Adam Gordon who has encouraged me all the way and whose proof reading is most gratefully acknowledged, and Alan Kirkman for reading the drafts of the book and correcting mistakes, adding information, and suggesting further areas to explore.

I would like to thank them all.

Finally to Elaine, my long suffering wife, who bears with great fortitude my hopeless mess and spending time writing when she knows I could be doing far more useful things.

Key to Abbreviations

ABS	Automatic braking systems	LRTA	Light Rail Transit Association
ACT	Aberdeen Corporation Tramways	LT	London Transport
AEI	Associated Electrical Industries	MC	Metropolitan-Cammel
AM&B	American Mutoscope & Biograph Co, USA	McGuire	McGuire Manufacturing Company, Chicago, USA
Balt	Baltimore Car Wheel Company, Baltimore, USA	MCTD	Manchester Corporation Tramways Department, Hyde Park Works
BCT	Blackpool Corporation Tramways, Rigby Road Depot.	ME	McHardy and Elliott Company Ltd, Edinburgh
BelCT	Belfast Corporation Tramways, Sandy Row Depot.	M&G	Mountain & Gibson Ltd, Bury
		M&T	Maley & Taunton Ltd, Wednesbury
BEC	British Electric Car Company Ltd, Trafford Park, Manchester	MET	Metropolitan Electric Tramways Ltd
BMR	Brecknell Munro & Rogers, Bristol	Milnes	Geo F Milnes & Co. Ltd, Birkenhead (subsequently at Hadley, Shropshire)
Brill	J.G. Brill Company, Philadelphia, USA	Milnes Voss	G.C. Milnes, Voss & Co. Ltd, Birkenhead
Bristol	Bristol Wagon & Carriage Works Ltd, Brislington Works, Bristol.	MT	Maximum Traction
		nc	New controllers
Brush	Brush Electrical Engineering Co. Ltd, Loughborough	NCT	Newcastle Corporation Tramways
		PAC	R. Y. Pickering and Co. Ltd, Wishaw
BTH	British Thompson Houston Co. Ltd, Rugby.	PE	Petrol-Electric
CCT	Coventry Corporation Tramways.	Peckham	Trucks built by or for the Peckham Truck & Engineering Co. Ltd. Most post-1908 Peckham trucks were built by the Brush Electrical Engineering Co. Ltd
CEM	Compagnie Electro-Mécanique, Switzerland		
CET	Coventry Electric Tramways		
CP	Crompton Parkinson, Bradford	Preston	21E type truck made by Dick, Kerr & Co. Ltd, Preston
Cravens	Cravens Railway Carriage & Wagon Co. Ltd, Darnall, Sheffield	Rad	Radial
DCT	Darwen Corporation Tramways	Raworth	Raworth's Traction Patents Ltd, Manchester
DK	Dick, Kerr & Co. Ltd, Preston		
ECT	Edinburgh Corporation Tramways	RCT	Rochdale Corporation Tramways
EE	English Electric Co. Ltd, Preston.	rm	Re-motored
EHC	Electricite & Hydraulique de Charleroi et Belge, Belgium	Roberts	Charles Roberts & Co Ltd, Horbury Junction, nr Wakefield
EMB	Electro-Mechanical Brake Co. Ltd, West Bromwich	Roe	Charles H. Roe Ltd, Leeds
		RYP	R.Y. Pickering Ltd, Wishaw
ER&TCW	Electric Railway & Tramway Carriage Works Ltd, Preston	s	Reused equipment from scrapped cars
		SCT	Sheffield City Tramways, Queens Road Works
GE	General Electric Company of America	SHMD	Stalybridge, Hyde, Mossley & Dukinfield Tramways & Electricity Board, Tame Valley Works
GEC	General Electric Company, Britain		
GCT	Glasgow Corporation Tramways		
Glouc	Gloucester Railway Carriage & Wagon Co. Ltd, Gloucester	SMW	Service Motor Works, Belfast
		SSCT	South Shields Corporation Tramways, Dean Road Workshops
Hill	W & E Hill Ltd, South Shields		
HF	Heenan Froude, Worcester	STD	Standard 21E type truck
HN	Hurst Nelson & Co. Ltd, Motherwell, Scotland	Steph	John Stephenson Company, New York, USA
IT	Imperial Tramways Co. Ltd	UCC	Union Construction and Finance Co. Ltd, London
J T Clark	J T Clark, Aberdeen		
Lancaster	Lancaster Railway Carriage & Wagon Co. Ltd, Lancaster	UDC	Urban District Council
		UEC	United Electric Car Company Ltd, Preston
LCC	London County Council	WH	British Westinghouse Electric & Manufacturing Co., Trafford Park
LCT	Leeds City Transport		
LF	Leeds Forge Co., Bristol		
LivCT	Liverpool Corporation Tramways	Witting	Witting Bros, London
LGOC	London General Omnibus Co., Chiswick	WS	Wilson & Stockall, Joinery Works, Rochdale Road, Bury
LNWR	London & North Western Railway		

Bibliography

BOOKS

The Westinghouse Company Annual Catalogue 1886, reprinted by Floyd Clymer, Los Angeles.

Report of the Special Committee appointed to consider the question of Brakes on Tramcars, published by the Municipal Tramways Association, 1903.

The Electric Tramcar Handbook by W.A. Agnew, published by H Alabaster, Gatehouse & Co. Third edition, 1905.

ICS Reference Library No. 186, Electric Railways, published by International Correspondence Schools Ltd., 1908.

ICS Reference Library No. 22, Construction and Equipment of Electric Tramways and Railways Electric Signalling on Railways, published by International Correspondence Schools Ltd., 1909.

Electric Traction by A.T. Dover, published by Sir Isaac Pitman & Sons Ltd, second impression, corrected, 1919.

A Life of George Westinghouse by H.G. Prout, published by Benn Brother Limited, 1922, reprinted by Kessinger Publishing, c.2004.

Progress in Electric Railway Transportation, published by Westinghouse Electric and Manufacturing Co, 1927.

The Trafford Park Works of Metropolitan-Vickers Electrical Company Limited, Manchester, published by "Engineering", 1929.

Electric Traction by A.T. Dover, published by Sir Isaac Pitman & Sons Ltd, second impression, revised and largely re-written, 1929.

ICS Reference Library No. 22D, Construction and Equipment of Electric Tramways and Railways Electric Signalling on Railways, published by International Correspondence Schools Ltd, 1937.

BTH Reminiscences Sixty Years of Progress by H.A. Price-Hughes, published by The British Thomson-Houston Company Limited, 1946.

1899 – 1949 Metropolitan Vickers Electrical Company by John Dummelow, published by Metropolitan Vickers Electrical Company, 1949.

Great British Tramway Networks 3rd Edition by W.H. Bett & J.C. Gillham, published by Light Railway Transport League 1961, revised as a series of booklets published by Light Railway Transport League from c.1975 to date.

Engineering without Wheels by Norman Swindin, published by Weidenfeld and Nicolson, London, 1962.

Light Railways of the First World War by W.J.K. Davies, published by David & Charles, 1967.

Trafford Park Tramways by Edward Gray, published by The Oakwood Press, 1964.

Anatomy of a Merger by Robert Jones and Oliver Marriott, published by Jonathan Cape, 1970 and Pan Books, 1972.

Transport Treasures of Trafford Park by Dennis Gill, published by The Transport Publishing Company, 1973.

Vickers Against the Odds 1956/77 by Harold Evans, published by Hodder & Stoughton, 1978

Westinghouse Electric Railway Transportation, Bulletin 118 of the Central Electric Railfan's Association, 1979.

EMB Trams by Andrew Young, published by Light Rail Transit Association, 1985.

Narrow Gauge at War by Keith Taylorson, published by Plateway Press, 1987.

Trafford Park Tramways 1897-1946 by Ted Gray, published by Northern Publishing Services, 1996.

Narrow Gauge at War 2 by Keith Taylorson, published by Plateway Press, 1996

My Fifty Years in Transport by Anthony George Grundy, published by The Tramway and Railway World Publishing Co. Ltd, 1944, republished by Adam Gordon, 1997.

Trafford Tramways by Arthur Kirby, published by Triangle Publishing, 2003.

Images of England Trafford Park by Karen Cliff and Pat Southern, published by Tempus Publishing Limited, 2003.

FILMS

Westinghouse Powering the Future, films of the main works at Pittsburgh taken in 1903, DVD produced by A2ZCDS, 2004

MAGAZINES ETC

Light Railway and Tramway World

Light Railway and Tramway Journal

Tramway Review

Modern Tramway

Tramway and Railway World

British Westinghouse and Metropolitan-Vickers publicity brochures

Adam Gordon
Transport Books

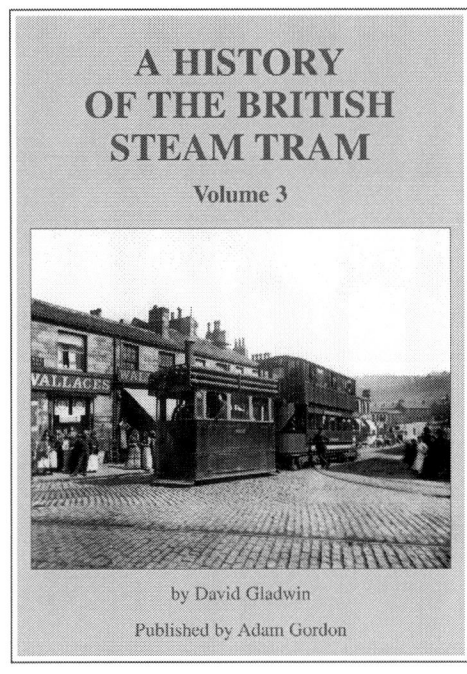

telephone
01408 622660

e-mail
adam@ahg-books.com

website
www.ahg-books.com

New Titles Projected for 2008

Life of Thomas Telford, reprint of his 1838 autobiography, together with album of copper plates.

Volume 4: A History of the British Steam Tram, D. Gladwin.

Volume 5: A History of the British Steam Tram, D. Gladwin.

British Tramways Bibliography, D. Croft and A. Gordon.

British Tramcar Manufacturers – British Westinghouse and Metropolitan-Vickers, D. Voice.

The Engineering Exploits of John Barraclough Fell, K. Pearson.

The Wearing of the Green, second edition, W. Tollan.

British Tramway Accidents, F. Wilson, edited by G. Claydon, laminated hardback, 228pp, £35

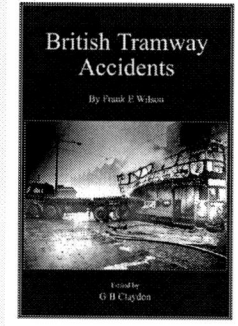

The Life of Isambard Kingdom Brunel, by his son, reprint of the 1870 edition, softback, 604pp, £20

The Cable System of Tramway Traction, reprint of 1896 publication, 56pp, softback, £10

The Definitive Guide to Trams (including Funiculars) in the British Isles, 3rd edition, D. Voice, softback, A5, 248pp, £20

The Development of the Modern Tram, Brian Patton, hardbacked, 208pp, profusely illustrated in colour, £40

Double-Deck Trams of the World, Beyond the British Isles, B. Patton, A4 softback, 180pp, £18

Double-Deck Trolleybuses of the World, Beyond the British Isles, B. Patton, A4, softback, 96pp, £16

The Douglas Horse Tramway, K. Pearson, softback, 96pp, £14.50

Edinburgh Street Tramways Co. Rules & Regulations, reprint of 1883 publication, softback, 56pp, £8

Edinburgh's Transport, Vol. 2, The Corporation Years, 1919-1975, D. Hunter, 192pp, softback, £20

The Feltham Car of the Metropolitan Electric and London United Tramways, reprint of 1931 publication, softback, 18pp, £5

Freight on Street Tramways in the British Isles, David Voice, B5, softback, 66pp, £12

Hospital Tramways and Railways, third edition, D. Voice, softback, 108pp, £25

How to Go Tram and Tramway Modelling, third edition, D. Voice, B4, 152pp, completely rewritten, softback, £20

London County Council Tramways, map and guide to car services, February 1915, reprint, c.12" x 17", folding out into 12 sections, £8

Metropolitan Electric, London United and South Metropolitan Electric Tramways routes map and guide, summer 1925, reprint, c.14" x 17", folding out into 15 sections, £8

Modern Tramway, reprint of volumes 1 & 2, 1938-1939, c.A4 cloth hardback, £38

My 50 Years in Transport, A.G. Grundy, 54pp, softback, 1997, £10

Omnibuses & Cabs, Their Origin and History, H.C. Moore, hardback reprint with d/w, 282pp, £25

The Overhaul of Tramcars, reprint of LT publication of 1935, 26pp, softback, £6

Next Stop Seaton! – Golden Jubilee History of Modern Electric Tramways Ltd., D. Jay & D. Voice, B5 softback, 136pp, coloured covers, £17

The History and Development of Steam Locomotion on Common Roads, W. Fletcher, reprint of 1891 edition, softback, 332pp, £18

The History of the Steam Tram, H. Whitcombe, hardback, over 60pp, £12

A History of the British Steam Tram, Volume 1, D. Gladwin, hardback, coloured covers, 176pp, 312 x 237mm, profusely illustrated, £40

A History of the British Steam Tram, Volume 2, D. Gladwin, hardback, size as above, coloured covers, 256pp, £40

A History of the British Steam Tram, Volume 3, D. Gladwin, hardback, size as above, coloured covers, 240pp, £45

Street Railways, their construction, operation and maintenance, C.B. Fairchild, reprint of 1892 publication, 496pp, hardback, profusely illustrated, £40

Toy and Model Trams of the World – Volume 1: Toys, die casts and souvenirs, G. Kuře and D. Voice, A4 softback, all colour, 128pp, £25

Toy and Model Trams of the World – Volume 2: Plastic, white metal and brass models and kits, G. Kuře and D. Voice, A4 softback, all colour, 188pp, £30

George Francis Train's Banquet, report of 1860 on the opening of the Birkenhead tramway, reprint, softback, 118pp, £10

My Life in Many States and in Foreign Lands, G.F. Train, reprint of his autobiography, softback, over 350pp, £12

The Tram Driver, by David Tudor, hardbacked, 72pp, £20

Trams, Trolleybuses and Buses and the Law before De-regulation, M. Yelton, B4, softback, 108pp, £15

Tramway Review, reprint of issues 1-16, 1950-1954, A5 cloth hardback, £23

Tramways and Electric Railways in the Nineteenth Century, reprint of Electric Railway Number of Cassier's Magazine, 1899, cloth hardback, over 250pp, £23

Tramways – Their Construction & Working, D. Kinnear Clark, reprint of the 1894 edition, softback, 812pp, £28

Life of Richard Trevithick, two volumes in one, reprint of 1872 edition, softback, 830pp, £25

The Twilight Years of the Trams in Aberdeen & Dundee, all colour, A4 softback, introduction and captions by A. Brotchie, 120pp, £25

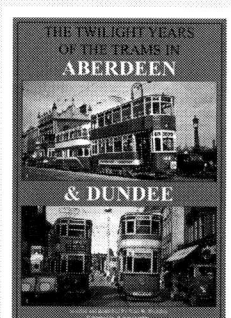

The Twilight Years of the Edinburgh Tram, A4 softback, includes 152 coloured pics, 112pp, £25

The Twilight Years of the Glasgow Tram, over 250 coloured views, A4, softback, 144 pp, £25

The Wantage Tramway, S.H. Pearce Higgins, with Introduction by John Betjeman, hardback reprint with d/w, over 158pp, £28

The Wearing of the Green, being reminiscences of the Glasgow trams, W. Tollan, softback, 96pp, £12

TERMS OF SALE

RETAIL UK – for post and packing please add 10% of the value of the order up to £4.90 maximum, orders £50 and over post and packing free. I regret that I am not yet equipped to deal with credit/debit cards.

RETAIL OVERSEAS – postage will be charged at printed paper rate via surface mail, unless otherwise requested. Payment please by sterling cash or cheque, UK sterling postage stamps, or direct bank to bank by arrangement.

SOCIETIES, CHARITIES etc. relating to tramways, buses and railways – a special 50% discount for any quantity of purchases is given provided my postal charges are paid.

WHOLESALE (TRADE) DISCOUNTS FOR MULTIPLE COPIES OF THE SAME TITLE
post free – details are available from Adam Gordon.

Adam Gordon Books
Kintradwell Farmhouse
Brora
Sutherland KW9 6LU